THE
YOUNG HISTORIAN

THE
YOUNG HISTORIAN

BY

N. H. BRASHER

Senior History Master, Bexley Grammar School

OXFORD UNIVERSITY PRESS

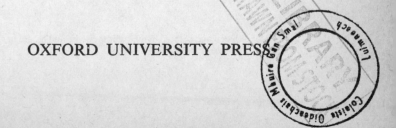

Oxford University Press, Walton Street, Oxford OX2 6DP

OXFORD LONDON GLASGOW
NEW YORK TORONTO MELBOURNE WELLINGTON
KUALA LUMPUR SINGAPORE JAKARTA HONG KONG TOKYO
DELHI BOMBAY CALCUTTA MADRAS KARACHI
IBADAN NAIROBI DAR ES SALAAM CAPE TOWN

For Robin and Martin, young historians

Reproduced and printed by photolithography and bound in
Great Britain at The Pitman Press, Bath

PREFACE

Those with first-hand experience of the Sixth Form History work, whether as teachers or students, will know that it demands much more than a retentive memory for factual knowledge, useful though that is. The ability to analyse subject-matter, to be relevant, to form sound judgements, and to express ideas well, is certainly no less important if the student is to make the best use of his knowledge. The object of this book is to help students in the development of these skills. They are not easily taught since the speed at which pupils master them is much more variable than the speed at which they master facts. A book which supplements class teaching, and from which the student can learn at his own pace will, I hope, be useful.

For the most part, examples used to illustrate the ideas are taken from the seventeenth to the twentieth centuries, the period most familiar to me in my teaching experience. The book has been written as an accompaniment to the whole of the two year A Level course, beginning with the basic training in style and selection of material needed by the new entrant into the Sixth Form, and ending in the last section (The Historian's Art) with work which is suitable for the very good A Level, or scholarship, candidate. In the sections on Style and Content the more sophisticated ideas appropriate for the Upper Sixth student, such as the chapters on Width and Depth, and on Judgement, have been kept to the end. The Lower Sixth student will, no doubt, stray into these chapters sometimes. They will do him no harm; if they interest him this suggests his readiness to absorb the ideas they contain.

My intention in the first part of the book is to help the student to construct a soundly based style for himself by showing specific techniques in writing; numerous examples are given from the work of modern historians. This emphasis on modern practice in historical writing is deliberate. Stylistic habits vary from age to age. Gibbon's style, for instance, is often admired, perhaps a little automatically, but it would be as absurd to imitate his style of writing now as to imitate his dress. If students were to learn to model their style on the work of the many outstanding modern historians who take pains to express themselves well, this would mark a substantial advance, not least in saving future generations of readers from the monumental and pointless boredom which might otherwise be inflicted on them. Content, rather than style, is the subject-matter of the second part of the book. Methods which help the student to analyse and organize his material are described in detail. Regular essay-writing is a basic feature of school and university courses in history; a methodical approach to the collection of material saves the student's time and energy. The final part of the book consists predominantly of a series of case-studies of the work of distinguished historians, past and present, in which extracts from their works are given accompanied by a critical commentary and questions. The object is to show how the standards of literary and historical judgement described in the earlier parts of the book can be applied to the writing of all historians however distinguished. The final extracts typify the work of students themselves, revealing the strengths and weaknesses which are apt to emerge in the essay work of young historians.

Much of this book was written during a sabbatical term made possible by the generosity of the Master, the Right Honourable Sir Frank Lee, G.C.M.G., K.C.B., and Fellows of Corpus Christi College, Cambridge. Their hospitality and friendly interest in the writing of this book were an invaluable stimulus to me. I owe, too, a debt of specific thanks to Professor C. R. Cheney, F.B.A., and to Dr. C. M. Andrew, both of Cambridge University. Their wide knowledge helped to make the extracts in the book much more representative of historical work than they would have been otherwise. I wish also to express my thanks to the Education Committee of the London Borough of Bexley who granted me leave of absence from my teaching post. As ever, I owe a debt of gratitude to my wife whose speedy and efficient typing was but one of innumerable ways in which she helped the production of this book.

CONTENTS

ACKNOWLEDGMENTS

We are indebted to the following publishers and authors for granting permission to quote extracts from their works:

Simon and Schuster Inc.: E. Gibbon, *The Decline and Fall of the Roman Empire.*

Longmans, Green, and Company: Lord Macaulay, *Critical and Historical Essays,* J. A. Froude, *History of England,* G. M. Trevelyan, *Garibaldi,* N. Gash, *Mr. Secretary Peel* (and for this book the Harvard University Press also).

John Murray: J. L. Motley, *The Life and Death of John of Barneveld.*

Macmillan and Company: R. W. Church, *Saint Anselm,* H. R. Trevor-Roper, *The Last Days of Hitler* (and for this book Harold Matson Inc. also).

Cambridge University Press: F. W. Maitland, *The Constitutional History of England.*

A. and C. Black: D. L. Keir, *The Constitutional History of Modern Britain 1485-1951.*

Constable and Company: J. Vincent, *The Formation of the Liberal Party 1857-1868* (and for this book Charles Scribner's Sons also).

And to Dame Veronica Wedgwood for an extract from *The King's Peace 1637-1641.*

Several briefer extracts from other books have been used; full details have been given about the publisher, author, and source in the text or in the footnotes.

SECTION I

STYLE

STYLE

The simplest approach towards the problem of style is to ignore it. 'Style is the man' runs the argument; why then should one interfere with nature? Besides, history is a specialist study. Even if it were conceded that a sense of style can be taught, there are some austere historians who are inclined to feel that history is too serious a subject to concern itself with literary niceties; for them, indifference to problems of style, far from being a product of mental laziness, is a positive historical virtue. With no siren sounds to divert him the historian can devote himself with single-minded zeal to the pursuit of truth. So it seems, firstly, that a sense of style cannot be taught, and, secondly, that even if it could it ought not to be. The argument has the attraction that it makes it positively virtuous to do nothing, a situation so unlikely in education that it makes the reasoning suspect.

Style in the writing of history is not, as has been suggested, a matter of indifference. Historians at every level are writing for an audience, and, if not, they ought to be. Certainly the central figure in this book, the young historian, knows very well that throughout his school and university career he will be presenting his work for judgement by others. Those who mark this work seek in it certain qualities—a power of analysis, a strong sense of relevance, a wide range of knowledge and the ability to integrate it in relation to the theme set; yet underpinning all these intellectual virtues is the sense of style which enables the writer to make the most of them. 'The purpose of literature is to give pleasure. The purpose of historical writing is to instruct. There is no reason why the two should not be combined ...' writes Dame Veronica Wedgwood,[1] whose own historical writing admirably proves the point.

[1] I. B. Newman (ed.), *English Historians* (Oxford University Press, 1957), foreword by Dame Veronica Wedgwood.

For all except a tiny minority of geniuses the acquisition of a skill, whether physical or mental, requires a detailed study of techniques. Some of the subtleties of style undoubtedly defy analysis; they are the product of individualistic inimitable experience. Teaching, therefore, has its limits; but what it can do is to transform a student whose writing is clumsy, colourless, and dull, into one whose writing is at least competent in a literary sense. The techniques which make this possible are studied in the following pages. Practice is of course essential; few history students are likely to feel any sense of deprivation in that respect.

1

SENTENCES

In some modern literature a sentence is merely a collection of words between two full-stops. Fortunately historical essays in the style of James Joyce are not yet in vogue; students mostly take the trouble to provide their sentences with subjects, verbs and punctuation. Yet, if that is the limit of their thinking on sentence structure, then their writing is less effective than it could be. One of the first structural considerations to bear in mind when writing is the length of the sentences used. It is temptingly easy to allow one's writing to drop into a regular pattern in which every sentence is almost precisely the same length. Over a page or two this method produces the soporific effect of a grandfather clock. A simple way of avoiding this monotony is to make occasional use of a short, or very short, sentence. This is particularly valuable when the writer wishes to give strong emphasis to an idea, nor does it require that laborious attention to literary detail which the young historian often suspects to be the aim of any attempt to improve his style. An awareness of the need to vary sentence lengths quickly becomes almost instinctive. It is a simple device. If there are any doubts about its value the following extract should help to dispel them.

The influence of Luther upon mankind was not restricted to that German and Scandinavian area which was permanently won for the Lutheran Church, but penetrated everywhere. His bold challenge rang through Europe. Was it true that the world had been treading a false road for more than a thousand years, that the Papacy was an imposture, the special sanctity of the priesthood a fiction, and that rites, ceremonies, and institutions interwoven with the familiar life of Europe were unnecessary and even harmful? Only the dullest indifference could fail to be startled by such a message. Opinions might differ as to its value. Some might think it very good, others wicked. But no one could deny that it was exciting.

H. A. L. Fisher, A History of Europe (Arnold, 1936), p. 541.

Obviously, if contrast can be secured by means of the short sentence it can be secured by means of the long sentence too, but this presents greater difficulties for the young writer. The long sentences he uses are sometimes so loosely organized that they part company with grammar, sense, and reader, long before they reach their overdue end. One antidote is the semi-colon. This breaks the sentence into compact units, giving both writer and reader a mental breathing space to grasp the development of the idea in easy stages. Students understand the value of this idea easily but then find that the use of semi-colons in practice is less easy than it first appears. Semi-colons scattered throughout an essay with nonchalant abandon will quickly reduce it to chaos. Discrimination is needed. One safe guiding rule is that phrases separated by semi-colons need to be closely connected in thought; the second phrase, for instance, may extend the idea contained in the first, or it may contradict it: but it must be connected with it. It follows from this that semi-colons can often be used as a substitute for conjunctions particularly by young students who tend to be over-generous with 'and' and 'but'. The risk of misuse by the novice is also reduced if he ensures that each semi-colon phrase is grammatically complete. Mature writers readily, and generally rightly, break all these rules but it is unwise to do so in the learning stage.

The semi-colon phrase, like the short sentence, can be used to round off a sequence of thought strongly. These two extracts show both usages at work.

Any future ruler would at his peril defy those whom Parliament represented: no ruler did. The King still retained considerable powers, within the framework of the rule of 'the free'. But the limits to the sovereign's power were real and recognized. William vetoed five Bills before 1696, but they all subsequently became law; after that date he used the veto no more. Anne's solitary veto in 1708 is the last in English history.

> C. Hill, *The Century of Revolution* (Nelson, 1961), p. 277.

During the siege of Oxford peers were two a penny in the overcrowded town, and hungry sentries on watch cried down to the besiegers: 'Roundhead, fling me up half a mutton and I will fling thee down a Lord.' Nor were things any better in London, where a miserable rump huddled, neglected and despised, in an empty House of Lords. In 1645 Lord Willoughby remarked bitterly, 'I thought it a crime to be a nobleman'; by the winter of 1648 there were only a handful of peers left to 'sit and tell tales by the fireside in their House in hope of more Lords to drive away the time'. A few months later the House of Lords was abolished, and with it the privileges which had hitherto helped to distinguish peers from gentry. This act was not a mere by-product of the dynamics of war; it was the culmination of a crisis of confidence which had been maturing for well over a half century.

> Lawrence Stone, *The Crisis of the Aristocracy, 1558-1641* (Oxford: Clarendon Press, 1965), p. 753.

Long sentences, controlled at tactical intervals by semi-colons or colons, can be useful in expressing ideas compactly, paradoxical though that may sound. There are occasions, even in the writing of major historical works, when there is a need for a brisk summing-up of the causes or consequences of an event; young historians who so often have to write timed essays have a greater need still to master the art of expressing a string of ideas concisely. A tedious catalogue of the 'firstly', 'secondly', 'thirdly' kind is too cumbrous. In contrast, this extract from a description by H. A. L. Fisher of the effects of the Black Death shows how deftly and concisely a wide range of information can be given by a well-controlled long sentence.

In England, perhaps, the changes were more noticeable than else-where: in the monasteries a marked decline in literary activity and discipline; in the impoverished country parishes empty rectories and absentee priests; in the grammar schools the substitution, with a new race of teachers, of English for French; in architecture the spread of the Perpendicular style, simpler than the older forms of Gothic, more easily standardized, and better adapted to the capacity of a diminished band of travelling masons; and finally, in agriculture a marked acceleration of that process of converting labour services into money payments, which led in time to the disappearance of an unfree village population, and to the break-up of the medieval system of tillage.

> H. A. L. Fisher, op. cit., p. 320.

The young essay-writer who has discovered the usefulness of the long controlled sentence or the emphatic effect which can be achieved by use of the short sentence sometimes over-uses them. Once they become predictable they cease to be useful. Contrast is the aim. Even in the simple matter of sentence structure there are several ways of avoiding a stereotyped approach. The obvious thought pattern, for instance, in constructing a sentence is to begin with the main clause and to continue with as many subordinate clauses as seem appropriate—not too many one hopes. This is a very reasonable arrangement so long as it does not recur in every sentence throughout the whole length of the essay; if it does the writing acquires a mechanical quality which eventually makes it very dull. Stimulating the reader's interest is not easy if every sentence has a regular pattern, and every reader deserves to be surprised occasionally. Varying the clause order is a simple but useful way of avoiding monotony, though, as with other techniques, over-use destroys its value. Macaulay's description of Frederick I of Prussia is an example of the way in which interest can be built up by delaying the main clause until almost the end of the sentence. 'Ostentatious and profuse, negligent of his true interests and of his high duties, insatiably eager for frivolous distinctions, he added nothing to the real weight of the state which he governed.'[1] Styles in writing change. Macaulay is often too wordy for modern tastes but this is not true of the extract given here: it is as sharply pointed a sentence as any modern historian could produce, and the word order is part of its strength. Modern historians make frequent use of the same technique. These two extracts from Maland[2] show the point. 'Her territories compactly joined, her land fertile and her population the largest of any European state, France was held back from pre-eminence in Europe only by the recurrent civil war and rebellion that had plagued her since 1559.' In the second extract the character of Harlay, Archbishop of Paris, is neatly pinpointed. 'Sufficiently scholarly to win attention, astute enough not to take his studies too seriously, he served Louis XIV with constant devotion and unflagging interest.'

A poverty-stricken vocabulary and stylistic carelessness can cause the young essay-writer to repeat identical words and phrases at such close quarters to each other that they have a jarring effect. Yet repetition, used purposefully, is a wholly different matter, strengthening not weakening expression. Macaulay's description of Prussia in the eighteenth century shows this method at work. 'In that spare but well-knit and well-exercised body, there was nothing but sinew, and muscle, and bone. No public creditors looked for dividends. No

[1] G. M. Macaulay, *Essays* (Longmans, 1883), p. 658.
[2] D. Maland, *Europe in the Seventeenth Century* (Macmillan, 1966), p. 237 & p. 254.

distant colonies required defence. No court, filled with flatterers and mistresses, devoured the pay of fifty battalions.[3] The metaphor at the beginning of the sentence is too fanciful, and the 'fifty' battalions mentioned at the end are more likely to be the product of Macaulay's imagination than of statistical evidence; but the emphatically repeated 'No' is worth attention as a means of emphasis.

There is no doubt that writing of this rhythmic kind does quicken the attention, though if it is used clumsily or too readily it becomes too artificial to maintain its effectiveness. There is, however, a more subtle way in which the writer can benefit from the instinct of readers to respond more attentively to ideas which have a rhythm of their own; this is by the balanced development of ideas so that a natural rhythm develops, in which words, phrases and sentences are set against each other. Historians have their own individual quirks of expression, but there is an area of common ground between many of them, and the neat organization of argument and counter-argument is a characteristic of those whose style makes their work rewarding to read. These extracts show how this 'rhythmic' writing stimulates interest, and gives added impact to the writer's ideas.

In fact much of Peel's weariness and irritation in the last phase of Wellington's ministry came from his sense of having responsibility without power. Not lack of policy but inability to make the Duke's cabinet the instrument of policy, was the root cause of his dissatisfaction. . . . The radical movement looked primarily to constitutional reform and a transfer of political power, and tended to assume that legislative benefits would automatically result from these changes. Peel, looking primarily to administrative reform, had no reason to think that organic changes in the constitution must necessarily precede, or indeed would necessarily assist, the new social and financial concepts to which he was moving. What the country needed, in his view, was more efficient government: the whole attitude of the radical opposition seemed to point towards less and more ineffective government.

N. Gash, *Mr. Secretary Peel* (Longmans, 1961), p. 669.

He was certainly against any large reconstruction of the representative system; equally clearly he was against the dead negation of Wellington and Ellenborough. He opposed the whig and radical demands not only because they went too far but also because he wanted to keep his hands free. But what he stood for, and what he

[3] G. M. Macaulay, op cit., p. 686.

would do if his hands were free, was not obvious to others and possibly not to himself.

N. Gash, op. cit., p. 672.

Often this sense of balance is achieved within a very few words. '(Louis XIV) was not a theologian, but he made up in prejudice what he lacked in understanding.'[4] 'Its armies (of the French Revolution) set out to revolutionize the world; its ideas actually did so.'[5] This balancing of sentences, and even of paragraphs, need not be a laborious, carefully contrived, piece of writing; it will have more force if it is not. It arises almost spontaneously for most historians simply because they are necessarily vigilant in their choice of words. If the historian has the active critical sense which one expects each idea, as it takes shape in his mind, is accompanied by its counter-idea, and by associated ideas. Sometimes he will reject these alternatives, sometimes accept them, sometimes modify them. He is in short acting as his own critic; this approach in itself encourages balanced judgement, and the balanced phrasing which accompanies it.

As with so many of the techniques of historical writing, once the writer becomes consciously aware of the value of a particular method it tends to be absorbed into his own repertoire. He then quickly passes to the stage where the particular technique such as balanced sentence structure and so on, becomes second nature to him. This enables him to concentrate on the content of the sentence more fully, confident in the knowledge that he has a sufficiently varied array of writing techniques at his disposal to be able to express himself well, whatever his subject-matter may be.

[4] D. Maland, op cit., p. 261.
[5] E. J. Hobsbawm, *The Age of Revolution* (Weidenfeld and Nicolson, 1962), p. 54.

2

WORDS AND PHRASES

1. *Concrete and abstract words*

Dislike for abstract terms, and for the pomposity of style which results from their too frequent use, is no novelty. Churchill's preference for words of Anglo-Saxon terseness, and Macaulay's use of concrete terms in passages of vivid description, these and many other examples, are part of a traditional English approach which can be traced at least as far back as Shakespeare. Since concrete terms are the natural form of expression, used from the time the child learns to read and write, one would expect the young historian to use them much more readily than abstract words; curiously, this is seldom so in practice. There is a middle-of-the-road quality about the vocabulary of many students. Lack of knowledge saves them from using the more ponderous abstractions which older historians sometimes inflict on their readers; yet, at the same time, they seem reluctant to use the concrete terms which would give more force to their writing. This may spring from the well-marked modern tendency to argue about problems in history rather than to describe events, so that the reader may rarely visualize the situation he is studying in terms of actions by human beings at all. The value of the concrete term is that it is a reminder that history does not consist simply of the arguments of historians; secondly, concrete terms enliven and strengthen writing. Not all historians, unfortunately, have the gift for expressing their learning vividly, but when they do have this capacity it is noticeable how often the concrete term gives force to their ideas.

Reference to the Industrial Revolution, for instance, could be made in this way:

'In the last part of the eighteenth century the cotton industry was the one most affected by the technical developments in production resulting from the Industrial Revolution. The extension of the factory system was a feature of economic change and led to a great expansion in the size of Manchester, for instance. The new methods of production had adverse effects upon living conditions there, but stimulated industrial activity and progress and, eventually, made Manchester so important that the views of the liberal economists known as the Manchester school acquired special significance, internationally, in economic thought.'

This is sound factually and shows an awareness of the historical significance of the events taking place, but the persistent use of abstract words robs the ideas expressed of much of their impact. The use of a few concrete words to describe the same events makes a striking difference, as the following extract shows.

Whoever says Industrial Revolution says cotton. When we think of it we see, like the contemporary foreign visitors to England, the new and revolutionary city of Manchester, which multiplied tenfold in size between 1760 and 1830 (from 17,000 to 180,000 inhabitants), where 'we observe hundreds of five- and six-storied factories, each with a towering chimney by its side, which exhales black coal vapour': which proverbially thought today what England would think tomorrow, and gave its name to the school of liberal economics that dominated the world.

> E. J. Hobsbawm, *Industry and Empire* (Weidenfeld and Nicolson, 1969), p. 40.

A second example of the forceful expression which the use of concrete terms makes possible comes from R. J. White. He is describing the reforming zeal of Joseph II of Austria.

Nothing was safe from the Emperor's levelling and economical hands, from the flogging rights of noble landlords to the wild boars they hunted and the gala days which delighted their ladies. He even told his loyal subject, Wolfgang Amadeus Mozart, not to put so many notes into his music. He wanted his subjects to enjoy themselves in the Prater and at the theatre. He wanted them to be happy.

> R. J. White, *Europe in the Eighteenth Century* (Macmillan, 1965), p. 213.

A. J. P. Taylor is another modern historian who makes use of the precise mental image which the concrete phrase creates in the reader's mind. Writing about Lloyd George he says, 'There was in him a strange mixture of resolution and timidity. His shirt, as he came to make a speech, was always wet through from nervous anxiety. Though Lloyd George often provided leadership of great moral courage, he trembled before he acted.'[1]

There are occasions which the experienced historian senses when, after a long period of explanation perhaps, the essential point needs to be emphatically made: the concrete term is a very good means of doing this. Each style of writing, however, has its weaknesses. Too great a partiality for abstract terms leaves the reader bored. Too great a fondness for concrete terms leads to an affected, over-dramatic approach which may become irritating. The aim, as with all stylistic devices, is to use them rationally, and not to allow any one of them to outstay its welcome.

2. *Metaphor and simile*[2]

Writers who visualize past events in terms of mental pictures of situations find it almost as natural to use metaphors and similes as it is to use concrete terms. Much depends on the writer's habits of thought. There are several excellent historians who make virtually no use at all of metaphors or similes. More than that, the academic historian is a little wary of them. These devices involve the use of the imagination; they are unreal in that they compare fact with fancy instead of fact with fact; they cannot be verified; one's concern should be with the subject-matter itself—the event or character-description—and not with comparisons which, however vivid, take the reader's mind a stage further away from reality. But if these criticisms are unquestioningly accepted, if metaphors and similes are to be as religiously avoided as if they were the work of the Devil, if historical writing consisted merely of strings of facts and ideas expressed as prosaically as possible, then history would be duller and more uninstructive than many writers have allowed it to become. Colourful expression of ideas does not rob them of their value as evidence. Consider for instance the way in which historical ideas are strengthened by the use of metaphor and simile in the following examples.

[1] *English History 1914-45* (Oxford: Clarendon Press, 1965), p. 73.
[2] Figures of speech comparing one thing with another. A simile is introduced by the words 'as', or 'like'.

Frederick the Great aspired to a place not inferior to that of the sovereigns of England, France, and Austria. For that end it was necessary that Prussia should be all sting.

G. M. Macaulay, op. cit., p. 686.

England was, in 1830, like a wide-spreading plain flooded with stagnant waters, which were the cause of malaria and distress. Railways were a grand system of drainage, carrying away to the running streams or to the ocean, the redundant moisture, and restoring the country to fertility and prosperity.

R. J. Baxter, *Journal of the Statistical Society, XXIX,* 1866.

The great frozen ice-cap of the world's traditional agrarian systems and rural social relations lay above the fertile soil of economic growth.

E. J. Hobsbawm, op. cit., p. 149

His impact (Peter the Great's) upon Muscovy, it has been said, was like that of a peasant hitting a horse with his fist. The horse remained a Muscovite under the skin, but it was to answer with increasing alacrity to the name of Russia.

R. J. White, op. cit., p. 77.

Ideas expressed in this way are apt to linger in the mind longer than if they were expressed more conventionally. Some writers seem unable to express their thoughts by use of metaphors, and they therefore have to emphasize their ideas by other means. Others, however, have a strong pictorial, comparative sense and to them the art of using metaphors presents little difficulty. Many can develop the skill once they realize its usefulness, and once they realize that it is not beyond their wits to create metaphors and similes themselves. Mistakes will be made, and the young historian needs to be warned off developing a flamboyant style, but by studying historical writing he will notice the way in which occasional metaphors and similes help the writer to achieve additional impact when he wants it.

3. *Paradox*[3]

Paradoxes are rare in historical writing and would lose their

[3] Expression of an idea in a contrary way to that expected.

value if they were not. The concentration of knowledge and critical reasoning to be found in paradoxical writing cannot be sustained over even a short period of writing, such as an essay; even if it could, it would defeat its own ends by over-burdening the mind of the reader. The mind, like the body, has a limited digestive capacity, and no one over the age of ten wants Christmas pudding all the time.

The ability to express an idea paradoxically comes from a questioning state of mind which accepts no statement automatically at its face value. The vigilant writer has an instinctive distrust of conventional statements about the past. In a sense the more agreement there is, the more he distrusts it. This attitude may lead him to use statements which are paradoxical, though in practice the writer is less concerned with the literary form than with modifying an impression which is strongly held merely because it has been repeated so often. Paradoxes of this kind are apt to arise naturally in the writing of historians of this calibre. Brief illustration of paradoxical writing is virtually impossible since the paradox by its nature is unlikely to be self-explanatory, and may need several pages of writing to justify it. The young historian, with little opportunity for the detailed first-hand research which can lead to a paradoxical approach, is still capable, however, of producing the paradoxical phrase. These phrases occur too in the work of senior historians. C. Hill, for instance, examining the way in which even in the Commonwealth period in the seventeenth century the wealthy still managed to maintain possession of the land writes succinctly that 'The rich inherited the earth.'[4]

If a young historian has a critical and observant approach there is no reason at all why he should feel that the paradoxical phrase is too sophisticated a literary device for him to use. The creation of a paradox is a by-product of a vigilant mind, and senior historians have no monopoly in that respect. Paradoxical contrasts of nouns and adjectives, for instance, of the kind achieved in phrases such as '*the malignant good fortune* of the birth of a posthumous child of the Duc de Berri', 'Louis Philippe's policy was *peaceful, commercial, and boring*' require a technique of expression which is not beyond the powers of students.

[4] Op. cit., p. 151.

4. *Economy of style*

Whether the student's pen is racing frenziedly across the page in an examination room, or moving hardly less slowly as he tries to meet a miscellany of demands for weekly or fortnightly work, he is continually engaged in private races with the clock. The most essential training of all in this respect is that he should learn to express his ideas compactly. Sometimes, the highlights of writing— the use of metaphor, paradox, and so on—may save him a host of humdrum phrases, but at the same time there are less spectacular parts in essays, whoever writes them. Passages of narrative or explanation are inevitable, but they can be word-wasting.

One of the simplest ways of avoiding this weakness, and the one most often used, is to preach the gospel of clarity. 'Be clear'. 'Be concise'. Or, a little more constructively, 'Be grammatical'. More constructively still, 'Don't let your sentences ramble on for too long.' The humorist has his own small quota to add. 'Say what you mean, and mean what you say.' 'If you have nothing to say don't say it' (dangerous advice!). These suggestions, for the most part, are sound enough as general propositions, but they are not particularly helpful in detail, they have lost much of their effectiveness through endless repetition, and there is the feeling that they represent the limits of the speaker's thinking on the subject. The section on sentence structure has dealt with many of the points raised in this flow of well-meaning advice, but there are a few other practical points to consider in developing an economical style of writing.

Padding has to be avoided, whether it is the major padding of irrelevance, or the minor padding of an over-wordy style. Young writers, once they get to the stage where they are capable of looking at their own work critically, often find that they have accumulated a number of favourite stop-gap words whose presence merely weakens the impact of their style. 'In fact', 'definitely', 'however', 'nevertheless', 'moreover'—these are examples of words which occur far more readily than they need. 'And' can be used too frequently. A useful experiment for a young writer is to read through his essay to see the extent by which he can improve his style by substituting a full stop or a semi-colon wherever he has used 'and'.

The essayist cannot hope to match the full length descriptions of characters found in many books, since the essay style cannot be so leisurely. By use of brief remarks in parenthesis, however, he can enliven references to those whose names appear in his writing. 'Courageous, aggressive, conscious of a sense of mission, confident that "the ship which carried him could never sink", Gustavus Adolphus erupted upon northern Europe like some half-forgotten volcano.' Sentences of this kind are worth the attention of young historians, since clauses in parenthesis if they are well-selected and neatly used quickly indicate the writer's knowledge. If he is sufficiently well-informed to be able to use this technique about some of the less well-known characters of history this gives the reader, or examiner, a useful insight into the depth of knowledge of the writer, without any need for the latter to write out lengthy character studies. Remarks in parenthesis are also valuable in giving the historian the chance to make brief, and preferably pungent, comments on the course of events he is describing. A. J. P. Taylor, for instance, in writing about the negotiations which preceded the General Strike of 1926 comments that 'The miners would not give way until the owners had done so—and perhaps not even then.'[5] Young writers may need to be warned not to preface every remark in parenthesis by a dash; this habit becomes as tedious as the prolific italics in Victorian letter-writing. Commas are often sufficient to rope off the remark in parenthesis. Sometimes a complete sentence may be parenthetical. J. H. Plumb's devastating description of the stupidity of George III is an instance of this. 'Had he been born in different circumstances it is unlikely that he could have earned a living except as an unskilled manual labourer.'[6]

Economy of style, as the examples show, does not mean a bare framework of words stripped of interest; what it chiefly requires is the ability to pack a large volume of critical judgement into a small space.

5. *Vocabulary*

One of the most useful by-products of the extensive reading undertaken by all historians should be a growth in vocabulary. The result should be an increased power to express finer shades of meaning in the historian's own writing. In practice this power of learning by observation and imitation is less successful than it ought to be.

[5] Op. cit., p. 243.
[6] *Men and Places* (The Cresset Press, 1963), p. 34.

Unconsciously, for the most part, the Sixth Former by his reading gradually enlarges his vocabulary so that it becomes wider than it was in his middle school years; but it is generally not much wider. The reason for this comparative failure lies in the mental inertia to which we are all liable. Technical words are not so numerous in history as they are in scientific subjects, and it is often possible to grasp the sense of a passage of historical writing without specific knowledge of the meaning of the few technical terms which the historian employs. It is therefore easy for the young historian to allow his mind to slip round phrases such as 'clericalist opposition', 'dynastic wars', 'rigidly mercantilist policies', without detailed understanding of their meaning. This debars him, or should do so, from using these phrases himself. Yet there are many phrases of this kind which are part of the normal vocabulary of the adult historian. Without them communication would be clumsy and slow; development of an idea would be paralysed if the writer had to stop to explain words such as 'prerogative', 'bureaucracy', 'legislature', in the course of his argument. There is, of course, a dividing line between choice of the right technical word, universally acceptable among historians, and the use of technical jargon, where the writer deliberately chooses obscure terms in order to appear learned. Nevertheless, there is undoubtedly a store of specialist words in common use in history which the young historian needs to acquire. Explanation by teachers will remove some of the difficulties, but more important, in the long run, is the recognition by the pupil himself of the tendency of the mind, like water, to follow the line of least resistance. Once he has understood this natural weakness there is more hope that the young historian will be sharply observant of the vocabulary used by adult historians; then he will rapidly reach the stage where he can absorb their language intelligently into the vocabulary which he uses himself.

Indifference to detail is not only a bar to sound history: it is also a bar to good writing. As will be seen later much more is involved in the creation of a good style of essay writing than the cultivation of a good vocabulary, but words are the tools of the job, and the student with a wide vocabulary has at least a potential advantage over one who has not. Sensitivity to words does not always come as a gift from nature and, even if it does, intelligent observation of the way in which most established historians express themselves extends the young student's own powers of varied and sharp expression. The phrase which appears on countless Sixth Form reports that 'He should read more widely' would be more specifically useful if it were replaced by the advice that 'He should read more observantly.'

In building up a vocabulary by conscious effort in this way there is of course a danger that the young historian, with the solemnity which the young sometimes have, will fall into the trap of invariably preferring the pompous to the simple word. If he has a feeling for words this is unlikely to happen; if he has not then he needs to remind himself, or be reminded, that the object in writing is not to stun the unfortunate reader with a barrage of ponderous words. Sir Arthur Quiller-Couch's advice that the writer should call a spade a spade and not an agricultural implement is still a useful corrective, though not if it leads to the writing of essays consisting exclusively of Anglo-Saxon monosyllables; that way boredom lies too. The extracts which follow, from the works of well-known historians, give some indication of the way in which the experienced writer can profit from the extensive vocabulary at his disposal. The passages do not represent particular high-lights in writing: they merely indicate the normal style of these authors, but the varied vocabulary, precise use of words, the occasional technical term, and the deft indication, sometimes by a single adjective, of the author's own judgement of the episodes he, or she, is describing, all give some insight into the way in which knowledge of words helps the writer to express ideas without pomposity but with authority. The words and phrases unlikely to be found in the writings of most Sixth Form historians have been italicized.

The *romantics* . . . condemned the laws and definitions pursued so *inexorably* by preceding generations as *bumptious* attempts to reduce a mysterious universe to the limits of men's *paltry* intelligence. Their bugbear was Newton whom they regarded as the *founding* father of the age of reason. To the *mechanistic* interpretations advanced by *Newtonian* science they opposed '*a natural philosophy*' which was emotional and *intuitive*, expressing the unity of all creation and the force of *the world spirit*. Yet despite much *unintelligible rhapsodizing* the basic desire of the romantics was plain to all: the wish to assert the overriding importance of individual personality.

Irene Collins, *The Age of Progress* (Arnold, 1964), p. 271.

Yet independence in a member of parliament must always be personal rather than *institutional*: even the county member ceased to enjoy his *proud immunity* from political intrigue if he had ambitions and abilities. . . . Dowdeswell, from independent Worcestershire, once he dreamed of office, could no longer avoid the practical bargains of professional politicians. But few county members were men of such ability. In Somerset even lords or the sons of lords were *anathema* to *a sturdy squirearchy* who sought a good back-bench man not of the front rank socially or politically.

To some extent the influence of London and its cultural predominance *sweetened the asperity* of the representatives of the independent squirearchy. To come to Westminster and be *cajoled* by lords and secretaries of state must have made some *backwoodsmen* less wilfully blind to the needs and desires of the executive.

> J. S. Watson, *The Reign of George II* (Oxford: Clarendon Press, 1960), pp. 62-3.

The *archpriest* of the new Crusades was Louis Kossuth, whose brilliant powers as orator and journalist, first directed towards securing the substitution of Magyar for Latin in the Hungarian Diet and afterwards *deployed* in a passionate campaign for Hungarian independence, awoke in every part of Europe *the latent flames of a furious and disruptive racialism*. By the spring of 1848 this powerful *demagogue* had been for eight years preaching his radical and nationalist doctrines to assemblies of his haughty and *tempestuous* fellow-countrymen.

Upon a government *thus corroded and assailed* the shock of the February revolution in Paris fell with a shattering force.

> H. A. L. Fisher, *A History of Europe* (Arnold, 1936), p. 920.

The words chosen in these extracts are not pretentious, but sometimes they are unusual, sometimes they are expressions of critical judgement, sometimes they are the necessary technical words. Good scholarship candidates can write in a near approximation to this style, but more by instinct than design perhaps. Yet any Sixth Former, once he develops an eye for detail, has it within his power to make his vocabulary the flexible and powerful ally which it becomes for the experienced historian.

Since history is, in part, a literary subject the potential vocabulary of the historian is as extensive as the dictionary itself. It would be impossible therefore to try to compile a common vocabulary of words which can be effectively used in general historical writing. Each historian, young or old, amasses his own selection from his own observation. On the other hand, history has its own specialist terms, knowledge of which is common ground among historians; without this knowledge effective reading and writing on the subject are impossible. The young historian does not always readily understand this. He needs to realize, for instance, that the term 'absolutism' is as useful to the historian as 'copper sulphate' is to the chemist. As an indication of the meaning of a specialist vocabulary in history a few examples are given here: obviously there are many more, but those chosen will be sufficient to show the student the kind of semi-technical term which arises in history.

Words associated with the exercise of power: autocratic, authoritarian, autonomous, hegemony, despotism, monarchical, absolutism, oligarchy, junta, aggrandisement.

Words associated with ecclesiastical history: clericalism, schismatic, ultramontane, temporal, secular, dissenter, simony, pluralism.

Words associated with governmental organization: bureaucracy, fiscal, mercantilist, cameralism, impeachment, jurisprudence, federal, executive, legislature, judiciary.

Words associated with intellectual movements: scholasticism, rationalism, romanticism, enlightenment, humanism, radicalism, utilitarianism.

Other examples could well be taken from foreign terms which the historian finds useful: *de facto, status quo, rapprochement, Realpolitik*. Others involve the use of adjectival words derived from names—Petrine Russia, Francophile, Physiocratic influence, Newtonian physics, Benthamite methods of administration. Many words and phrases owe their origin to particular historical circumstances—a policy of 'blood and iron', the West Indian lobby, the 'window on the west' policy of Peter the Great. Each particular period, each particular country, will have its stock of words of this kind, well known by all adult students of the period concerned. No historian could write with much confidence about the history of Britain in the 1830s, for instance, unless he were thoroughly familiar with the meaning of freeholders, copyholders, hearth tax, Benthamism, Boards of Guardians, deterrent principle, Speenhamland, and so on.

There are, in short, scores of words which the adult historian uses readily, but which the young historian can only absorb and use as a result of observation and effort. In return for his effort he gains greater flexibility in style, and growing confidence in his own ability to write history well.

6. *Common errors*

The emphasis in a book on style ought to be constructive; consequently only incidental reference has been made so far to the weaknesses of expression which occur in students' writing. Nevertheless, a brief collective indictment of a number of common faults may be a useful guide for the student analysing his own style, particularly in his first year in the Sixth Form, the formative stage when the O Level caterpillar is changing into the A Level butterfly. The older student is, or should be, less likely to make the blatant blunders described below; his primary concern in style should be to develop by imitation and experiment the more advanced techniques of expression described elsewhere in this book.

Among the most frequent errors are these:

(a) *Colloquialisms* These are expressions which may be acceptable in conversation but which are out of place in essay writing. *Examples:* 'to be really hard up'; 'things began to look up'; 'the next question that crops up'; 'a great deal of'; 'a lot of'; 'he realized that this had just got to be changed'; 'don't' (for 'do not'), and similar contractions.

(b) *Clichés* Sometimes clichés appear in the form of a noun accompanied by a stock adjective. *Examples:* 'ruthless determination'; 'wily diplomat'; 'considerable importance'; 'outstanding ability'. These, and many others, have all the boredom of the expected. Sometimes clichés consist of metaphors whose freshness has been lost by too frequent use. *Examples:* 'this point of view'; 'an iron hand in a velvet glove'; 'a will of iron'; 'the root of the trouble'. Historical phrases can become clichés. *Examples:* 'Bonny Prince Charlie'; 'Le Roi Soleil'; 'more royalist than the King'; 'a reign of terror'; 'the Little Corporal'.

(c) *Word-wasting* This may be produced by mechanical use by the writer of individual words which reduce the impact of the sentence without adding to its meaning. There are occasions when the words mentioned in the list which follows are essential in a sentence, but it is instructive to see how often they can be missed out with advantage. *Examples:* 'obviously'; 'clearly'; 'really'; 'definite(ly)'; 'actual(ly)'; 'in fact'; 'somewhat'; 'rather'; 'quite'; 'of course'; 'moreover'; 'furthermore'; 'nevertheless'; 'however'; 'also' (particularly ugly at the start of a sentence); 'the' (as in 'the Parliament'); 'just' (he just wanted); 'in conclusion'; 'finally'. Another form of word-wasting occurs in the habit of some students of using verbs, nouns, or adjectives, in pairs where the second half of the pair adds virtually nothing to the meaning of the first half. *Examples:* 'to develop and improve'; 'to fight and struggle'; 'to organize and arrange'; 'strength and power'; 'a policy of fraud and deceit'; 'headstrong and impulsive'. Word-wasting may arise through loose expression of ideas. *Examples:* 'There was more than one problem, in fact there were several'; 'With regard to Germany generous terms were needed but they were not given to Germany in case she became strong enough to make war again'; 'on the question of German participation at the Peace Conference the peace-makers cannot be blamed for ignoring that'. Thoughtlessness likewise leads to word-wasting in the use of non-functional adjectives such as 'a new innovation', and 'a good improvement'.

(d) *Weak or clumsy phrasing* 'Factor' and 'aspect', over-used words, are apt to produce sentences such as 'The next factor to consider is Frederick II's handling of foreign affairs.' Sentences of this kind are not wholly wasted. They indicate the writer's intention, but it is often possible to do this and to develop the theme simultaneously. An experienced writer makes the transition in argument more smoothly. He might begin a new paragraph, for instance, by writing 'Frederick's foreign policy was characterized by a similar opportunism'. Clumsy expression occurs frequently at the beginning of paragraphs when the writer is introducing a new stage in the argument. *Examples:* 'On the foreign policy side'; 'As regards foreign policy'; 'In the field of foreign policy'; 'The foreign policy aspect grew in importance during the reign'. The better writer is more direct. He might introduce similar subject-matter on foreign policy in this way. 'The attempts to westernize Russia made necessary a policy of territorial expansion.' Among the more elementary mistakes which produce weak expression are the use of abbreviations (e.g., etc.), and the use of numbered lists, in describing the causes of historical events, for instance. This latter usage may show that the writer has remembered his notes well, but it shows nothing of his literary or historical skill. Numbered lists are useful in note-making, and they are sometimes justified in books, but in a historical essay where the essence of the matter is to test the writer's ability to integrate his knowledge in the development of a strong argument the enumerated list is out of place. The split infinitive, a notorious example of clumsy phrasing, should be avoided too. Very occasionally its use may be justified if neater expression can be secured by splitting the infinitive than by not doing so, but it is more useful for the student to be aware of the ugliness of phrasing which is the usual result of splitting the infinitive ('to religiously try'; 'to more successfully resist').

(e) *Absolute words* The use of these and similar words—no, all, only, always, never, unique—is frequently a mark of the student's limited knowledge. Trained historians, conscious of the great extent and diversity of history, are more wary in their use of absolute words. They are generous, when the sense makes it necessary, in the use of qualifying words, 'most', 'almost', 'rarely', and so on. When students do make a mistake of this kind it often springs from using a specific fact from a limited period as if it had universal validity. *Example:* 'Coke was the first person to attempt enrichment of his land.' Absolute words are also used to limit unjustifiably the range of argument. *Example:* 'The only option available to Catherine was to over-issue paper currency.' A similar misuse of absolute words occurs when students are careless or gloss over difficulties. *Examples:* 'No mechanical tools were being manufactured to help the (early nineteenth-century) farmer in his plight.' 'All the major European powers in 1740 intended to take advantage of Austrian weakness.' 'The doctrine of collective responsibility ensured that the Prime Minister always had to have full Cabinet support in policy decisions.'

(f) *Grammar* By the time a student has reached the Sixth Form his work ought to be free from elementary grammatical errors, otherwise he has no foundation on which to construct an effective style. Much students' work, however, has to be written at great speed, and under pressure errors occur. One common fault in these conditions is to write pseudo-sentences in which faulty punctuation leads to a break-down of the sentence structure. Phrases in apposition are sometimes misused in this way, the phrase being wrongly treated as if it were a sentence in itself, 'The first of these being a necessary preliminary to good farming.' is an instance of a pseudo-sentence, taken from an essay on nineteenth-century farming. Another frequent error is to provide a multiple subject with a singular verb. 'The power and skill of the Prussian army *was* shatteringly evident at Sadowa.' Misused sentences produce ambiguity. 'The Polish Constitution allowed the existence of a Diet, and there was an elective monarchy. *This* made *it* weak.' Seldom, one hopes, does so short a sentence create such confusion. Grammatical mistakes otherwise tend to be as varied as the individuals who make them. Often it is a matter of a student developing a blind spot over an elementary grammatical rule although his work is grammatically sound in general. The misuse of apostrophes is an instance of this type of mistake; students cannot always distinguish between 'labourer's' and 'labourers'', or 'it's' and 'its'.[7] The racy style to be heard at times in journalism and television may have disconcerting effects on the grammar of students lacking literary sense; the increasing use of 'quote' for 'quotation' illustrates the point. Misunderstanding of grammatical rules can lead to ambiguity which has its lighter side for the examiner though not for the candidate. To be told that 'Columbus discovered America sailing westwards across the Atlantic Ocean', or, in an essay on nineteenth-century industrial development, that 'hosiery continued to grow' unintentionally creates bizarre mental pictures for the reader.

(g) *Spelling* Inaccurate spelling is a more frequent fault than poor grammatical construction. Dictionaries provide a partial remedy, as do books which examine awkward spellings of plurals, past tenses, and so on. The difficulty in practice is that it is only the occasional perfectionist who is going to break off his sentence in mid-flight in order to go and check the spelling of a word. Checking essays through at the end is an obvious alternative, but this means two re-readings, one to check facts and the development of the argument, and a second to check details of expression and spelling. This may often be a counsel of perfection. Pressure of work, and the student's unawareness of his uncertainty over the

[7] Students who find grammatical problems difficult will find abundant help in H. W. Fowler, *A Dictionary of Modern English Usage* (Oxford: Clarendon Press, 1954).

spelling of isolated words, make it unlikely that he will give much time to patient checking from dictionaries of possible spelling mistakes. Wide and observant reading is the most realistic method of preventing spelling mistakes, and this will generally be usefully supplemented by the marker's corrections. It may, however, be of some value to students to know the kind of words in which spelling mistakes occur. The modest list which follows, shows words frequently used in history essays which are apt to be misspelt. *Examples: Double letter difficulties*—commission, committee, amenities, amendment, immigrant, emigrant, skilful, successful, professional, deficient, disadvantage, dissatisfied, aggression, exaggeration, benefited, profited, tariff. *ie/ei*—received, believed, grievance, yield, siege, seize.

The 'i before e except after c' rule is a slight help but as in all English spelling learning by looking rather than reliance on mechanical rules is the best habit for the student to acquire.

Sound and spelling—separate, existence, independence, principle, warrant, salary, pursuit, troops, stabilize, governor, responsible, competent, tenant, bureaucracy, led, paid, representative, affected, effected (the meanings of these last two are also often confused. 'Affected' means 'influenced'; 'effected' means 'accomplished').

In these examples the student who relies on his hearing of the spoken word, rather than on his observation of the written one, is apt to make spelling mistakes since in speech the vowel sounds are so often slurred. Dependence on hearing produces mistakes in the choice of consonants too. The following list shows some words where this kind of error occurs.

Government, criticize, quarters, acquire, debt, influential, conscientious, decision, practice (noun), practise (verb).

Speech habits can lead to the omission of letters or to the intrusion of superfluous ones. In the list which follows the common mis-spellings are shown in brackets.

Hindrance (hinderance), development (developement), Elizabethan (Elizabethean), privilege (priviledge), monasteries (monastries), Emperor (Emperor).

Students have varying degrees of spelling blindness; to be free of the weakness altogether is a rarity. It is not invariably the most able who are the best spellers but they tend to be, suggesting that there is an extra sensitivity to detail in their reading which may benefit their work in other ways too. Knowledge of Latin is of occasional assistance in spelling correctly but does not provide entirely reliable guidance, particularly over words which appear to be derived directly from Latin but which have in fact passed through French first before being incorporated into the English language. The word 'tenant' is an instance of the way in which knowledge of the Latin source alone would lead to a mis-spelling of the word. Extensive reading is so intrinsic a part of the work of the young historian that familiarity with the written word gradually removes most of the weaknesses in spelling from which he may suffer at first. At least he should be able to avoid the disastrous blunder of a middle schoolpupil who wrote that 'Peter the Great was very badly educated and his spelling was atroshus.'

3

QUOTATIONS

There are rare occasions when a historian is writing about events which he has seen himself, but normally he sees his facts through the eyes of others. He will use whatever contemporary documents he can find and he will also be influenced to some extent by the ideas of other historians. As a result his work is apt to be sprinkled liberally with quotations as he indicates the sources of his facts and ideas. The young historian is quick to imitate this scholarly habit, though not always for scholarly reasons. At its worst the use of quotations can become a mechanical exercise, a pretentious display of name-dropping. Sometimes quotations are used as a smoke-screen to disguise the inadequacy of the writer: sometimes they are used as a weak gesture of deference to authority, inspired by a dim awareness that, as better historians than the writer use quotations, he ought to do so too; at least he can imitate that virtue in their writing, or so he thinks.

Fortunately there are better reasons, both historical and literary, for the use of quotations than these. A quotation, especially from a contemporary source, may be more illuminating than many pages of explanation. In a fifth century decree, for instance, issued by the Council of Toledo, there is a section which deals with the punishment of wives who have sinned. 'The husband' it commands, 'is bound to chastise his wife moderately, unless he be a cleric, in which case he may chastise her the harder.'[1] Twentieth-century readers, thoroughly accustomed to the equality of the sexes and the declining influence of the Church, suddenly find their minds transported to a society whose values were very different from their own. Or, suppose that the writer's intention was to describe the almost ruth-

[1] G. C. Coulton, *Medieval Panorama* (C.U.P., 1945), p. 615.

less curiosity which was a characteristic of the intellectuals of the Renaissance, could he find a better way of doing so, in brief, than this passage from Erasmus' *Ratio*?

'The student should learn to quote Scripture, not second-hand but from the fountain-head, and take care not to distort its meaning as some do, interpreting the 'Church' as the 'clergy', the 'laity' as the 'world', and the like. To get at the real meaning, it is not enough to take four or five isolated words; you must look where they come from, what was said, in other words, what preceded, what followed.'[2]

Quotations of this kind, which ideally combine both insight and brevity, are invaluable to the writer of history essays, with little time for leisurely exposition. In examinations, where the pressure of time is greater still, the quotation from Erasmus, for instance, is a little long to be accurately memorized, but the last sentence of the quotation would be sufficient to convey the essential point clearly.

Ideally, quotations should be in the language used by the original speaker, or writer, but this is a counsel of perfection, and it will only rarely happen that the central idea contained in a quotation will suffer much loss by translation. Nevertheless, if the young historian in the process of quoting occasionally burst into French, German or Latin, it will do his writing no harm since it will show a respect for original sources, and, equally importantly, by giving variety and unexpectedness to his writing it will make it of greater interest. Once the novice had grasped the value of quoting from original sources he can then begin to use quotations with discrimination, since they are plainly not all of equal value. It is better, for instance, to give a description of Frederick the Great's character based on his own comments, rather than on the over-digested opinions of generations of text-book writers. 'Frederick II earned a reputation for untrustworthiness' is the kind of sentence which may occur in a score or more text-books. It may be a sound opinion but, as it stands, it is merely a flat statement backed by nothing more than the weight the reader happens to attach to the authority of the author. Quotations of this kind do nothing to increase the merit of an essay because they show neither scholarship nor distinction of expression. On the other hand, if the same idea is

[2] E. E. Reynolds, *Thomas More and Erasmus* (Burns and Oates, 1965), p. 109.

expressed in Frederick's own words in his *Memoirs*, 'La méfiance est la mère de la sûreté', the idea immediately becomes more valuable, partly because it is from an original source, partly because it gives a revealing insight into Frederick's character and the political situation of eighteenth-century Prussia. It has the further merit of a good quotation that it can be used as a decisive summing-up of a series of comments by the writer—the *coup de grâce* to round off an argument strongly; alternatively, it is sufficiently provocative to be the starting-point of a sequence of ideas inspired by the quotation itself.

In attaching so much importance to contemporary quotations there is a danger of accepting them uncritically. 'Reading,' said Bernard Shaw, 'made Don Quixote a gentleman, but believing what he read drove him mad.' Comments from contemporary diaries, letters, memoirs, books, newspapers, and speeches, to name some of the obvious sources, can be historically valuable provided that the student knows the prejudices of the writer or speaker; in practice, this is extremely difficult even for the professional historian, but if the young historian learns not to believe all that he reads, however exalted the source, and if he approaches source material with as much background knowledge and common sense as he can bring to bear, then the risk of his treating contemporary sources with exaggerated respect is greatly reduced. He will quickly learn, for instance, not to take on trust the memoirs of statesmen or soldiers, such as Bismarck or Napoleon, writing with a care for their own historical reputations. At a less obvious level he may wonder how far T. E. Lawrence's judgement of the Peace Conference handling of the Arab-Jew question after the 1914-18 war was influenced by the part Lawrence himself played in helping the Arabs to fight their way through to Damascus. In these and a whole host of other instances the writer has to make up his mind to what extent he can accept the evidence of contemporaries; refusal to accept opinions at their face value is an essential part of the discipline of history.

This does not mean that quotations from prejudiced sources can never be used. They show something of the nature of a Bismarck or a Napoleon, for instance, even if their opinions are warped. Then, too, contemporary quotations reflect something of the times in which they were written; even the most skilful manipulator of facts cannot falsify every fact on which he comments. Some sense of the atmosphere of the age, and even something of the truth, will emerge from the most prejudiced account, if it is carefully studied. Besides, not all sources are equally polluted. Presumably, for instance, Samuel Smiles was writing without intent to deceive when he said, 'The healthy spirit of self-help created amongst the working-people would more than any other measure serve to raise them as a class, and this, not by pulling down others, but by levelling them up to a higher and still advancing standard of religion, intelligence, and virtue.'[3] Surely it is possible to see in this quotation some of the assumptions on which some Victorians based their view of society. Historical training encourages scepticism but one has to be prepared to recognize that writers have frequent bouts of honesty; sometimes the face value of a quotation may prove to be its only value.

The use of lengthy quotations to make more vivid a dramatic scene is more likely to be found in books than in essays, since in the latter there is greater emphasis on analysis and less on narrative. Long extracts such as Motley's description of the execution of John of Barneveld, or Elizabeth's speech to the troops at Tilbury in 1588, or Cresacre More's account of the trial of Sir Thomas More, can scarcely be included in full in an essay. In matters of this kind the art of the essayist lies in making the significant short extract. So often in a dramatic event the atmosphere and clash of personalities create a heightened intensity of mind and emotion which cuts away inessentials and exposes the fundamental thought and character of those concerned. It is as if, in a crisis, one or other of the leading figures finds by inspiration the words which show his whole character, and this is the material which the essayist seeks, brief and significant. An incident in Sir Thomas More's trial illustrates the point. Mr. Rich, giving evidence for the prosecution, reported to the court a conversation he had had with Sir Thomas, during which he alleged that Sir Thomas had denied the right of Parliament to accept the King as head of the church. Sir Thomas refused to accept this damaging evidence as an accurate report of the conversation. 'And if this oath, Mr. Rich, which you have taken be true then I pray that I never see God in the face; which I would not say, were it otherwise, to gain the whole world.' This one flash of indignant

[3] *Self-Help* (1859).

denial cannot express everything about Sir Thomas More's attitude at his trial, but it expresses much. Nowhere else, perhaps, in the trial are his devotion to God and his indifference to worldly advantage more compactly expressed.

Although quotations from public records have the advantage of being derived from an original source their value will vary. Statistics, for instance, are often unrevealing, partly because they are only concerned with information about facts which can be measured objectively. History is an art as well as a science, and is quite as much concerned with men's motives and attitudes as it is with their consumption of refrigerated beef, and other data respected by the statistician. Besides, statistics are notoriously unreliable before the twentieth century since information was often inexpertly and incompletely collected. Nevertheless, there are occasions when public records give a few solid stepping stones for the historian as he picks his way cautiously through the morass of misinformation about the past. At least it is certain that the Bill of Rights, for example, was passed, and that its terms are known. 'That the levying money for, or to, the use of the crown by pretence of prerogative, without grant of parliament, for a longer time, or in other manner than the same is or shall be granted, is illegal.' This quotation is specific, important, and from an authentic source; it is even reasonably clear, an unexpected virtue in a legal document. Apart from being a decisive landmark in the history of the relations of Parliament and the monarchy on the issue of raising taxation, this clause of the Bill is significant in the words chosen; 'by pretence of prerogative' uncovers in a phrase the hard feelings nursed by Parliament over James II's ill-timed attempt to revive the ancient powers of the monarchy.

Legislative enactments are thus a valuable source for quotations, but their value is greatly increased if the extracts from them are accompanied by intelligent comment. Dull in their wording themselves they give solidity rather than interest to historical writing, until the writer learns to develop his skill in selecting significant passages and in fitting in these passages neatly into the pattern of his argument. But, even when dealing with the apparently impregnable reliability of formal documentary evidence, the historian needs to keep his critical sense on permanent sentry-go. 'Medieval legislation was a pious aspiration', is an old tag, but it is almost equally true of later times until at least the middle of the nineteenth century. Knowing the laws is one thing, knowing whether they were put into practice is another. Even Frederick the Great, hardworking, efficient, dominant in Prussia as not even his father had been, could not get all his imperious orders performed. When one of his ministers died it was discovered that he had been regularly placing Frederick's edicts in a small box by his bedside with no intention of giving them any practical effect. Facts like this need to be known before any worthwhile judgement of policies can be made. Obviously quotations lose much of their effectiveness unless they are backed by a sound understanding of the period involved; the writer's comments on the quotation are no less important than the quotation itself.

Official records would be a tedious, though important, source of information if they consisted only of legislative enactments. Fortunately there is an abundance of alternative material. State trials of the sixteenth century, for instance, or the reports of the Commissions investigating working conditions in the nineteenth century, give many opportunities for interesting and significant quotation. The need for a revision of the hours of work for children in the nineteenth-century factories is vividly shown, for instance, in the evidence given to the Committee on Factory Children's labour 1831-2.

—Were children excessively fatigued by this labour?
—Many times; we have cried often when we have given them the little victualling we had to give them; we had to shake them, and they have fallen asleep with the victuals in their mouths many a time.

If quotations were to be arranged in order of value as evidence contemporary documents and accounts would head the list. Next in order would come the opinions of the specialist historians who have devoted themselves so fully to particular sectors of history that their judgements are acceptable in much the same way that the layman acknowledges the expertise of a doctor, dentist, or solicitor. Maitland on constitutional history, Namier on some aspects of the reign of George III, Holdsworth on English law, Clapham on economic history, spring to mind as examples of specialist writers whose works command respect of this kind. There are many others too; the young historian, looking for specific guidance on this matter, will find it by studying the bibliographies in the Oxford History of England and in the New Cambridge Modern History series.

In practice the greater difficulty for the young historian is to know what value to attach to the ideas he finds in text-books and journals whose authors are unlikely to be included in the bibliographies just mentioned. One view is to ignore text-books as sources of quotations altogether unless they are written by well-known specialists; they are not works of original research; they merely repeat knowledge, they do not add to it. There is an element of snobbery in this approach since even specialist authors derive many of their ideas from the work of others, as their footnotes show. Nevertheless, the young historian has to learn to live with life as it is, and he will generally be wise to avoid quoting directly from the little known authors whose text-books on English and European history appear so profusely in publishers' catalogues, and later in the schools themselves. There might be a case for quoting from them if their ideas are freshly expressed, even if the ideas themselves are not new, but this does not frequently occur.

Journals, as sources of quotations, set a different problem. Often the articles in them have the merit of being written by specialists, but they may have defects which mislead the uninitiated. There is a tendency, occasionally, for research students to write in a jargon which can only be understood by their fellow research students ('as bittern calls to bittern across the vasty deep'); sometimes, too, there is a feeling that some of the subjects discussed in learned journals would be of little consequence even if they could be understood. There are two dangers for the young historian in articles of this kind; he may respect the article beyond its merits because of its pretentious style; worse still, he may imitate it. Both these dangers can be avoided if he remembers that what he is seeking, both in quotations and in his writing in general, are ideas which are significant, understandable, and, if possible, well-phrased. If the specialist writers, however distinguished, fail in these respects then they deserve neither to be quoted nor imitated.

Once the quotations have been selected—and this should be a part of the preparation for writing—then consideration should be given to the ways in which they are to be blended into the essay. Variety gives interest, and to preface every quotation with the too familiar words 'As Professor Blank says ...', or to end every quotation with the name of the author in brackets is a dull-minded approach, which detracts from the value of the quotation. What is needed is intelligent comment on the quotation. It is more effective, for example, to write 'A. J. P. Taylor's assertion that "the Crimean War was the only successful invasion of Russia in modern times".[4] is a useful corrective to the many accounts of the war which treat it as the epitome of military idiocy' rather than merely to write 'As A. J. P. Taylor says "the Crimean War was the only successful invasion of Russia in modern times".' The second example shows that the writer is familiar with Taylor's idea; the first example shows that he has thought about it. Sometimes the result of this thought will be that the young historian will disagree, in whole or in part, with the idea contained in the quotation, though it may still be useful in advancing the argument in his essay. If he does disagree then so much the better. It shows that his mind is awake, and that he is not accepting the authority of the writer blindly: but he must show why he disagrees.

There may be some occasions when the writer has linked his ideas together so effectively that a quotation can be introduced without any need for comment. The quotation itself is then a natural step in the theme which he is developing. When this happens it is superfluous to introduce specific critical comment on the quotation: it is stronger if it stands alone. An essay on the 1848 Revolution in France, might with advantage be rounded off with Tocqueville's phrase, given without comment. 'The government was not overthrown; it was allowed to fall.' As another instance, a paragraph on religious feeling in Renaissance Italy could be very neatly concluded with Ariosto's devastating comment, 'Non credere sopra il tetto' (Their faith goes no higher than the roof).

Brevity, significance, striking phrasing, these are the chief needs in choosing quotations for history essays. If to these qualities the young historian can add some of his own—an understanding of the merits and defects of the various sources, a sense of relevance so that quotations drop neatly into place as he develops his ideas, a feeling for words so that quotations are not invariably introduced

[4] A. J. P. Taylor, *The Struggle for Mastery in Europe 1848-1918* (Oxford: Clarendon Press, 1954), p. 82.

with the same mechanical phrase—then quotations can powerfully reinforce his own writing; in studying critically their use he will see at first hand some of the problems which confront the professional historian.

4

INTRODUCTIONS AND
CONCLUSIONS

If historians were required to accept a self-denying ordinance by which their highest quality writing could only be allowed in two paragraphs of an essay or chapter, the odds are that they would choose the introduction and conclusion. There are good reasons for this. Every historian is writing for an audience, even if the audience only consists of one schoolmaster—or posterity—and this influences, in the first place, the style of introductions. The writer needs to make clear to his reader at the earliest stage what his main theme is to be; secondly, whether he wants it or not, his style will show the reader something of the quality of the writer's mind. The writer, after all, is inviting his reader to live with his thoughts for several minutes, and he ought to want to make the experience interesting as well as instructive.

Introductions are therefore of crucial importance. By the end of the first paragraph of an essay the reader will have a shrewd idea of what to expect in style, argument, and knowledge, in the rest of the essay. If he is confronted, for instance, with the following all too common type of introduction (in answer to a question on Joseph II's claims to be an Enlightened Despot) he will expect the worst.

'Before I examine the work of Joseph II it is necessary to give the background of Austrian history during the previous hundred years in domestic as well as foreign affairs. Austria, after the defeat of the Turks at Vienna in 1683 etc....' By the end of an opening paragraph of this type the reader—and Joseph II—will have been submerged in a flood of largely irrelevant detail. There is the added irritant that devotees of this humdrum approach often seem to have a special aptitude for bad spelling and indifferent punctuation—

a product probably, like their style, of unobservant reading. There are occasions, of course, when the historical background to a subject may make an excellent introduction. The trouble arises when this method is used mechanically, as it so often is, simply through ignorance of any alternative. A similar objection applies to the work of those students, determinedly logical, who develop an obsession in their introductions for defining words in the question. This is readily forgivable since at least it is some guarantee of relevance, but it can be clumsily used and, again, it is not always the ideal introduction for every subject.

Plainly, the major weakness of the types of introduction mentioned is their lack of variety and flexibility. There are, in practice, many variants possible; several of them are examined in the succeeding pages.

1. *Quotation*

The use of one or more quotations to set the tone of an opening paragraph is a common practice, and it can be strongly justified. The idea contained in the quotation will probably be strikingly expressed; it will also give some indication, one hopes, of the writer's reading and of his ability to recognize a significant phrase. Then, too, the young historian, when he uses a relevant, interesting, quotation from the work of an experienced specialist historian, has the encouraging feeling that the expert's judgement is adding to the weight of his own. If the quotation is taken from an original source—a parliamentary statute, a diary, or memoirs, for instance— it may make an even better starting point for the essay, since it suggests immediately that the writer prefers first-hand to second-hand history. There are thus several sound reasons for using quotations at such a crucial point in the essay as the introduction. There are dangers, too. One is the risk of over-use. The other, more dangerous still, springs from the habit of students of learning a number of quotations which they hope will be relevant in their examination papers; even if they are not relevant, optimistic students believe that they can be made to appear so with a little ingenuity: perhaps they sometimes succeed. Nevertheless, the introduction is the vital place, the power-house of the essay, where by one means or another the line of argument is being firmly indicated. The quotation which the young historian has carefully learned and treasured is particularly likely to be used in this early stage, when he is anxious to make an impressive start. But if he thinks in terms of using a quotation simply to make an impression rather than to attack the question, he runs the risk of introducing irrelevance from which it is difficult to recover. So long, however, as he uses that rare quality, common sense, he is unlikely to stumble into this trap.

Care should be taken over the way in which the quotation is introduced. To let it stand boldly alone as the first sentence of the essay is quite effective. Information about the speaker, or writer, and the circumstances, can be blended into the sentence which follows. Alternatively all this information can be grouped together into a single opening sentence. The two examples which follow suggest ways in which quotations can be used to launch essays, and also the way in which an idea can be developed, using a quotation as the basis.

Question: *What were the aims of Metternich in international affairs? To what extent did he achieve them?*

'L'Europe a pris pour moi la valeur d'une patrie.' Metternich's comment, made in 1824, was sentimental, for Europe was not a political entity, even in 1815 when the peacemakers banqueted so lavishly together in Vienna; with each passing year the Great Powers increasingly reverted to their eighteenth-century attitudes, more conscious of their mutual distrust than of any common aim. It is often said that Metternich wanted to put the clock back to 1789. Yet, when this was achieved in international affairs by the breakdown of the Congress idea, no one was more disappointed than he. In a sense his ideas belonged to a concept not then envisaged, of a United Europe; but, whether he wanted to go onwards towards that concept, or backwards to a Europe dominated by Church and Empire, there is no doubt that Metternich was out of tune with his times.

Question: *Discuss the effects of Frederick II's invasion of Silesia.*

Frederick's comment on the moral issues of the Silesian invasion was that, 'the matter of right is the affair of my ministers'. Certainly, the morality of the invasion is not the sole criterion by which it should be judged; but it was not so negligible in importance as Frederick seemed to think. By 1763 he could count his gains and his losses:

Silesia gained, 'the greatest permanent conquest of territory hitherto made by any power in the history of modern western Europe'; so Dorn describes it: but Prussia devastated, and the losses catalogued, with characteristic Teutonic thoroughness, down to the last pig in the Electoral Mark. What this precise catalogue failed to show was the distrust which Frederick's cynicism had created. Prussia had become the rogue elephant of Europe, a reputation which clung to it deservedly until 1945. In the long run bad morals make bad politics, and ultimately distrust of Prussian militarism was the most far-reaching consequence of the Silesian invasion for Prussia.

Other factors, besides the use of quotations, are involved in making these examples satisfactory as introductions, but they illustrate the way in which a quotation can trigger off a useful sequence of thought.

2. Historical background

Although introductions which give the historical background to a subject can be tedious and largely irrelevant, there are questions where the historical background is an essential part of the theme. Everything depends on the wording of the question, and the nature of the subject-matter. If the question were asked 'Does Catherine II of Russia deserve her title "the Great"?', there might well be numerous references in the introduction to the difficulties of Russia at home and her wasted opportunities abroad during the years immediately preceding Catherine's reign. The essay would then go on to show, by contrast, the achievements of Catherine. This would make a satisfactory introduction, but there are several other possibilities which might prove effective—the extent of Catherine's enlightenment, or the perpetual problems of governing Russia arising from that country's size and geographical position, or the relative strengths and weaknesses of the other Great Powers during Catherine's reign. If, to take another example, the question were 'Discuss the influence of nationalism upon European affairs from 1815 to 1848', it would plainly be pointless and time-wasting to use the introduction to discuss the growth of national consciousness in the eighteenth century. Such a leisurely pursuit of the question may be legitimate in a book; in an essay, particularly in an examination, time is too precious to be squandered in this way. Yet there are occasions when the historical background may provide the best possible introduction to an essay. If the question asked about Catherine II of Russia, were applied to Frederick William of Brandenburg, 'Does Frederick William deserve the title "the Great Elector"?', then it is difficult to see that one can do very much better in the introduction than describe the state of Brandenburg at the beginning of his period of rule; the greatness of Frederick William depends so much on the contrast between the state of his possessions in 1640 and their condition in 1688. The example shows one way in which this important theme can be firmly established from the outset:

In 1640, Frederick William, aged twenty, became the ruler of Brandenburg. His country was the helpless victim of foreign armies, still continuing the savage struggles of the Thirty Years' War. His own army consisted of a few hundred pillaging mercenaries. His small territories were bespattered across Europe from the Niemen to the Rhine; their soil was a patchwork of sand and bog. If greatness were to grow out of such beginnings it would need to be a very sturdy growth indeed. Yet, when Frederick William died in 1688, his organization of the administrative system and economic life of his country had created a solid basis for the later growth of the Prussian state. Moreover, in foreign affairs Brandenburg had won the respect of Europe in 1675 at Fehrbellin, first hint of Prussia's later military greatness, where the Swedish army had been shattered. These substantial achievements were largely the work of one man, Frederick William, rightly known to his subjects, even during his own lifetime, as 'the Great'.

Often, of course, the background information given will range over a longer period than in the example just given. An assessment of Luther's career, of Peter the Great's reforms, or of the causes of the World Wars of the twentieth century, would make necessary rather more concentration than usual, for instance, on the relevance of earlier events to the central issue being discussed. Each question has to be judged on its merits; the main point is for the writer to have a good array of introductory methods at his disposal so that he can make an intelligent choice.

3. *The link with political or historical theory*

In detail history does not repeat itself; in general terms it usually does. This is the basis of political and historical theory. Certain basic human problems recur whether the historian is writing about events in ancient Greece, or events in modern Britain, or about any other of the vast number of happenings in the history of the world. The distribution of power within the state, the attainment of liberty without licence, the maintenance of order without dictatorship, the motives for aggression in foreign policy, the problems of Empire, the influence of religious or political faith on human behaviour, these, and other issues of the kind, are part of the permanent subject-matter of history. Obviously it is easier for the older historian to see an event in its wider context in this way, as an instance of a general historical problem, than it is for the young historian with his narrower range of knowledge. Nevertheless, if the latter takes the trouble to study the ideas of political theorists such as Plato, St. Thomas Aquinas, Locke, or Hegel, and of historical theorists such as Tolstoy, or Toynbee, or of the numerous modern historians, with their cautious scientific approach, his capacity as a historian will be very usefully extended. He will gain greater understanding of the nature of the problems about which he is writing, and, with this, a detached approach which adds weight to his judgements. Within the narrow limits of an essay opportunities for direct reference to theory will be limited, but the introduction is clearly the section of the essay where background knowledge of this kind can most effectively be used. In the following examples the first one makes use of political theory to illustrate the theme; the second one uses historical theory.

Question: *Assess the contribution of Catherine II to the internal development of Russia.*

In Hobbes' judgement the first need of Society was order. Absolutism, preferably monarchical and based on a secular foundation, was the means by which this would best be accomplished. Hobbes' insight into the fundamental need of his times was shared by Catherine the Great a century later. Catherine's concept of her monarchical powers is much more closely akin to the ideas of the seventeenth century English political theorist than to those of the *philosophes* with whom she corresponded so frequently and to so little purpose. In theory, Catherine may have shared the enthusiasm of the French writers for the enlightened rule of a 'philosopher-king'; in practice, the ruler who consigned Alexander Radishchev to Siberia, because she disapproved of his criticism of peasant labour-obligations in his book *Journey from*

St. Petersburg to Moscow, was neither enlightened nor philosophical.

Question: *Discuss the significance in British constitutional history of the 'Glorious Revolution'.*

'There is,' wrote H. A. L. Fisher, 'only one safe rule for the historian: that he should recognise in the development of human destinies the play of the contingent and the unforeseen.'[1] Because 'the Glorious Revolution' is regarded, and rightly so, as a decisive landmark in British constitutional history it is easy, too easy, to read into the minds of the main actors intentions which were never there at the time. The actions of these men were not dictated by any strong consciousness of political theory, but by chance and opportunism, 'the play of the contingent and the unforeseen'. Their behaviour was largely conditioned by immediate reactions to immediate events—the evasiveness of Charles II, the tactlessness of James II, the risk of a sequence of Catholic rulers following the birth of a son to James' wife, the need of William of Orange for English men and money in his war against Louis XIV, and the well-founded English suspicion of the French King. These 'chance' elements influenced the nature of 'the Glorious Revolution' much more strongly than any coherent theory of the constitution; John Locke's theory of the contractual relationship between ruler and ruled was used to justify the Revolution not to inspire it.

4. Historical interpretations

History is constantly being rewritten. The versions of the past which satisfied our predecessors do not always convince us now, and, in due course a new generation of historians will criticize and amend the work of present-day historians. Some subjects have attracted particular attention in this way. New evidence, and new interpretations of existing evidence, have radically changed previous ideas about the three-field system, the causes of the French Revolution, and the effects of the Industrial Revolution, for instance. One of the most striking examples of all is the way in which so many different judgements have been formed of George III's views on his powers of personal government, particularly during the early years of his reign. On this subject there is a long sequence of argument and counter-argument beginning with the diary of Dodington published in 1783 and continuing through the nineteenth-century Whig historians to the scholarly researches of Sir Lewis

[1] Op. cit., Preface, p. v.

Namier and his followers, and then ending, at the moment, with the criticisms by Herbert Butterfield of some aspects of the Namier approach to the problem. Many subjects have become battlegrounds for historians in this way, but, unlike battles, historical arguments never end; at any time a skirmish, or a full-scale campaign may break out as the professional historians, reinvigorated with fresh evidence or fresh ideas, rush forth to do battle. Whatever the period which the young historian is studying it is likely that somewhere within his field of study there will be issues on which he needs to inform himself, or be informed, of a clash of historical opinion. A review of the different attitudes of historians, past and present, to the problem he is required to discuss may sometimes be a useful introduction in itself. It at least shows that the student is aware that more than one interpretation of events is possible, and it gives him an opportunity of exercising his judgement in choosing one interpretation rather than another.

The danger of this type of introduction is that the knowledge shown by the young historian is likely, at best, to be second-hand. He may know a potted version of the judgements of historians on the reign of George III, for instance, without ever having read any of them. Reference to them then becomes an exercise in name-dropping, and the lack of substantial knowledge of the work of the historian mentioned has a disconcerting knack of becoming apparent to the experienced reader. Nevertheless, there is another way, more honest perhaps and consequently more convincing, in which the young writer can convey his recognition of the way in which historical judgements can change, and this is by showing the variety of interpretation possible himself. This is not so difficult as it sounds. The example which follows shows one method of approach. The writer's views are not propped up by the names of authorities, but the opening paragraphs show the critical attitude which is an essential part of the historian's outlook.

Question: *Account for Henry VIII's breach with Rome*

Henry VIII, weary of Catherine of Aragon and of her failure to give him a male heir, and hoping for a better fortune with Anne Boleyn, was confident that his efficient servant, Cardinal Wolsey, would be able to persuade Pope Clement to annul the marriage with Catherine. That marriage had itself required a special Papal dispensation, since

Catherine was the widow of Henry's brother, Arthur. If the book of Leviticus had been more faithfully obeyed the marriage would never have taken place. Perhaps there was a curse upon it. Superstition, the King's inclinations, and the duty of providing for the succession, all pointed towards the need for divorce. The Pope, powerless to resist the Emperor Charles V, Catherine's nephew, desperately temporised. Tedious legal enquiries took the place of action until Henry, using the Reformation Parliament to give him moral support for his immoral behaviour, brought about the breach with Rome.

This familiar catalogue of the events leading to the setting-up of a state-dominated Church in England has the authority of the oft-repeated story. Like the oath used in courts of law it is supposed to contain not merely the truth but the whole truth; this, to a quite remarkable extent, it fails to do. In reality, Henry's breach with Rome was produced quite as much by the philosophers of Ancient Greece, by the Italian Renaissance, by Luther, by the political condition of Europe, and by the history of the Papacy, as it was by the attractive appearance of Anne Boleyn.

From this point the writer, having prepared the ground, can develop in detail his theme that Henry's actions were the result of an accumulation of long-term and short-term causes. The use of the 'tongue in the cheek' introductory paragraph to trace an interpretation which is faulty, followed by a second paragraph which abruptly changes course is a useful variant in introducing essays but it needs to be skilfully used.

5. *The arts*

Painting, architecture, sculpture, music, and literature, collectively and even separately, can often give a speedier and perhaps truer insight into the mood of an age than any public record. Reference to the arts is particularly appropriate in introductions, therefore, where the aim is to strike at the heart of the problem being discussed. The following example shows how a mind, receptive to the arts, can use them to illustrate an idea vividly.

A French cartoon of 1815 shows an eagle leaving the Tuileries, and five geese waddling in. The flight of Napoleon and the return of the Bourbons to the palace of their ancestors were symbolic of the great changes that were taking place from one end of Europe to the other during the years 1814 and 1815, and to a war-weary generation they were proof enough that the French Revolution had come to an end.

> F. B. Artz, *Reaction and Revolution 1814-32* (Harper & Row, 1934, p. 1).

A second example makes more detailed use of one of the arts as a means of showing the nature of an age.

Question: *'The ineffectiveness of the French monarchy after 1715 was the prime cause of the French Revolution.'* Discuss.

The weaknesses of eighteenth-century France can be seen as readily in its paintings as in its tax-returns, but the former are more pleasant to look at, and much more accurate. The French painters of the rococo period depict an escapist, aristocratic world, obsessed with the love of pleasure, graceful, charming, romantic, idle. Watteau's 'Embarkation for Cythera' could be its symbol—and perhaps its epitaph. There is a significant change also in the style of portraiture. In imitation of Louis XIV portraits had been formal, and designed to impress the viewer with the importance of the subject. Under Louis XVI, particularly, all this is changed. Portraits became casual and frivolous, symptomatic of the changing nature of the monarchy. Art was less centred on the King; so was France, and this was perhaps her misfortune. A resurrected Louis XIV might have averted the Revolution, but his successors were not of the calibre to do so.

6. *Definition*

Defining words and phrases in a question may be an essential deck-clearing operation in an introduction. Some historical controversies rest primarily on the use of words; the young historian, confronted with a question on the Industrial Revolution, the Age of Reason, Enlightened Despotism, or on other matters involving similar convenient but slightly misleading 'label' terms, is entirely justified in examining their precise meaning at a very early stage in the essay. It may be an obvious means of introducing the essay, but there are occasions when the obvious approach is also the best. Other questions, besides those involving the use of terms which have roused historical controversy, may also need to be approached by means of defining terms. If the question were 'Was Disraeli a politician rather than a statesman?' those two nouns need to be defined before progress can be made. On the other hand, there are questions where painstaking definition of obvious terms is merely superfluous. In answering a question such as 'What factors weakened

Sweden in the eighteenth century?' the writer has no need whatsoever in his introduction to discourse about what he means by 'weakened'. If he attaches to the word a meaning which has never been attached to it before then he is justified in explaining himself; but if he has every intention of using the word in the normal sense then he has no right to bore the reader with such an obvious fact.

7. *Specialized knowledge*

Specific interest in a particular branch of knowledge, not necessarily historical, may lead to the writing of an introduction which has all the impact of an original and well-informed approach. The arts have already been mentioned in this connection, but there are many other possibilities. The psychological approach to historical problems, although it is often distrusted because of the difficulty of finding trustworthy evidence to explain motives, ought not to be discounted altogether. A knowledge of some of the basic ideas of psychological theory would not necessarily be out of place in considering, for instance, how far Frederick the Great's behaviour was influenced by his upbringing, and would provide an interesting approach in an introduction. It is worth remembering, too, among those students who are nervous of writing anything which has not been written before that the essay, above all, is the type of writing which encourages brilliance and originality; the writer has to make a strong impact with his ideas, and the way in which he expresses them, in a short space of time. Specialized knowledge of an unusual nature is an excellent base from which this originality can develop. Work of this kind does stand out from the general mass of orthodox examination answers. The particular subject-matter in which an interest is developed does not greatly matter; an intense interest in modern transport methods may be as valuable as a similar interest in Mayan civilization. The nature of the question, and the ability of the student to see a relevance between his specialized interest and the problem being considered is the crucial matter. Economics, highly relevant for instance in questions on mercantilism and free trade, or local history, are examples of other branches of knowledge which may yield a fresh approach to a historical problem. Suppose, for instance, that the subject-matter of an introduction was to be the ignorance and superstition which forms an underlying theme of so much of medieval life. There are, of course, many ways in which this idea could be introduced but the following example shows how a knowledge of local history could make a useful starting-point.

If superstition has survived the onset of universal education and modern materialism—and there is no doubt that it has—it is not difficult to imagine what a potent force it was in the Middle Ages. Witchcraft, spells, and omens, were as real and as dangerous as death for medieval man. The educated classes often shared these fears. One medieval preacher argued that there will be more women than men in hell; women, in general, were better-behaved than men, but their great tendency to witchcraft would damn them. A more striking instance still of the irrational medieval outlook is to be found in a Northumberland assize roll of the thirteenth century. A man was accused before the court of killing a woman with a pitchfork. He excused his action by saying that she had cast a spell over him. The jury found his story so convincing that they brought in a verdict that he had killed the woman in self-defence against the Devil.[2] The common sense needed to create a society with some respect for justice struggled for long in vain against lunatic prejudice of this kind.

8. *Direct attack*

Introductions of this kind are brief, vigorous in style, and go immediately to the heart of the question. It might seem therefore that they would be the ideal start to any answer; in practice this is not always so. The swift 'direct attack' introduction is not necessarily suitable in answers where historical background has to be explained at some length, nor in answers where the issues are too wide, philosophical, or complex to be presented in a few incisive phrases. Besides, it would be dull-minded to use the same form of introduction monotonously when there are so many interesting variants possible. In examinations, for instance, the student will answer some four questions, and a stereotyped introductory method soon becomes apparent and boring. The 'direct attack' introduction, however, is particularly useful when the wording of the question invites an aggressively critical approach.

Question: *What is the importance of the reign of Louis Philippe?*

[2] G. C. Coulton, *Medieval Panorama* (Cambridge University Press, 1945), p. 117.

The reign of Louis Philippe was of no importance. It merely confirmed what Frenchmen already knew, and other Europeans feared, that Bonapartism was a virus from which the French have never recovered. This was suspected in 1814, confirmed in 1815 and 1830, and the diagnosis in 1848 was as superfluous as Louis Philippe himself. Examination of his reign in whatever sphere, foreign policy, social policy, constitutional organization, administrative system, economic management, merely underlines the obvious, that Louis Philippe, like his immediate predecessors and his many successors, could make no impact on the French people. The history of France between 1814 and 1958 is merely a long hyphen between Napoleon and de Gaulle.

9. *Anecdote*

Occasionally an incident occurs which epitomizes character or situation. Such an incident may very well provide the nucleus of an introduction. It would be difficult, for instance, to form a clearer impression, briefly, of the quality of Frederick II's leadership than in the story of his behaviour at Kunersdorf where striding about among his troops, like some irate but respected sergeant-major, he bellowed at them, 'Dogs! Would you live for ever?' Sometimes the incident may be less dramatic but no less revealing, as the following introduction shows.

Question: *'The weakness of the French system of government in the years before the Revolution of 1789 was not despotism but the lack of it.'* Discuss.

In 1787 Chateaubriand was formally presented to Louis XVI by Marshal Duras. He described the meeting in his memoirs. 'The King looked at me, returned my greeting, hesitated, and looked as if he wanted to say something. Then, more embarrassed than I was myself, finding nothing to say to me he passed on (on his way to mass).' France in the eighteenth century was a country which had the resources of man-power, natural products, and intellectual energy, to overcome with consummate ease the deficiencies of its revenues, but it needed firm leadership to do so. That there was little cause to expect such leadership from 'le grand timide' is strongly apparent in the brief encounter between Chateaubriand and his King.

The introductory methods described show something of the variety of approach possible, and may suggest means by which the student can avoid the mental blankness apt to come upon him as he casts around desperately for an effective opening paragraph. There are finally a few general considerations to bear in mind about essay introductions. They must be relevant since the approach adopted in the introduction normally dictates the pattern of thought throughout the rest of the essay. They ought to be relatively brief. The essay writer who gives a third of his space to his introduction is losing sense of proportion—and in schools or in examinations he will lose a large number of his marks as well. Finally, introductions should be interesting from the moment the reader starts to study them. This means, in practice, that the first sentence gives immediate insight into the writer's ability to handle words and ideas in an interesting way. A well organized opening sentence stimulates attention, a badly organized one kills interest from the start. The examples which follow show how some, at least, of the writers of history books are aware of the value of an interesting start; in essays, where ideas have to be concentrated into a short space, the need for a decisive beginning is even greater.

Each of the examples has been taken from the opening sentences of chapters in the books mentioned.

Europe is a peninsula at the north-western tip of Africa and Asia.

> R. J. White, *Europe in the Eighteenth Century* (Macmillan, 1965, p. 3.)

Until 1914 a sensible, law-abiding Englishman could pass through life and hardly notice the existence of the state, beyond the post office and the policeman.

> A. J. P. Taylor, *England 1914-1945* (Oxford: Clarendon Press, 1965, p. 1.)

The first thing to observe about the world of the 1780s is that it was at once much smaller and much larger than ours.

> E. J. Hobsbawm, *The Age of Revolution* (Weidenfeld and Nicolson, 1962, p. 7.)

Each of these sentences has a vividness and an element of surprise which immediately catch the reader's attention. The warning needs to be added that a brilliantly phrased opening sentence is of little value if the idea which it contains is not part of the pattern of argument being developed in the introduction; a paradox may provide an impressive start to an essay, but the writer then has to convince the reader that it is true.

Conclusions to essays provide less difficulty for young historians than introductions do. Occasionally, from shortage of time or knowledge, students omit conclusions altogether. This is irritating for the reader; moreover, it is a criticism of the writer if he finishes lamely without performing the necessary task of grouping his major ideas compactly together and making his answer to the question clear. One other suggestion may be useful in strengthening the conclusion to an essay, namely, that just as the first sentence is of particular importance in an essay so, too, is the last. A firm and interesting comment at this stage rounds off the theme strongly. The power to finish off a section of historical writing decisively is readily found among established historians, as the examples show. It springs from a strongly logical approach, combined with a sense of literary neatness.

The best known example of all perhaps is from J. L. Motley's *The Rise of the Dutch Republic*. He describes the assassination of William the Silent, and then finishes with this sentence: 'As long as he lived he was the guiding star of a whole brave nation, and when he died the little children cried in the streets.'

This comment, founded on a contemporary record, is direct, strong, and simple: though it may not appeal as a model to those who fear sentimentality? The writer, with an eye for metaphors may also find that literary device helpful in achieving a strong finish. Two examples from modern historians show this method at work. The first example consists of the closing sentence to a chapter on the political and religious restiveness of Europe in the seventeenth century.

In England, therefore, the storm of the mid-century, which blew throughout Europe, struck the most brittle, most overgrown, most rigid court of all and brought it violently down.

H. R. Trevor-Roper, *Religion, the Reformation, and Social Change* (Macmillan, 1967), p. 89.

In the second example the writer is rounding off an argument in which he has shown that during the 'Great Depression' in the last quarter of the nineteenth century new industrial growth was taking place, and the managers and organizers, in some industries at least, were not nearly so cautious and unimaginative as they are sometimes assumed to have been.

The problems of the entrepreneur were likewise not uniform: they varied according to the age and prospects of his industry. Averages and aggregates obscure such realities that derive from historic, social development. In short the British economy in these years was neither a stale egg nor a fresh egg. It was a curate's egg.

> C. H. Wilson, 'Economy and Society in Late Victorian Britain' (*Economic History Review*, 2nd Ser., XVIII, No. 1 (1965), p. 198.

A quotation if it is sharply expressed and relevant, may also provide an admirable end to an essay. Whatever method is used, the final sentence should give the same sense of completion as the builder feels when the last brick is set into its place.

5

WIDTH AND DEPTH

One of the less obvious but most telling ways in which the mature historian shows his skill is in the width as well as the depth of his knowledge. Of these two qualities the latter is the harder for the young historian to acquire. The professional historian has at his disposal time, opportunity, and the materials for research, on a scale much more lavish than that available for the young student. Inevitably the judgements of the young historian, even at scholarship level, will be based almost entirely on second-hand knowledge derived from teachers and books; the crowded academic curriculum of the Sixth Former, and even of the undergraduate, makes it impossible for them to devote their time to the close, leisurely study and comparison of original sources in which the professional historian can engage. The most he can generally expect to achieve, in terms of depth of knowledge, is to study the books of collected documents relating to his period, and to be alert to the possibility of using well-known contemporary memoirs and accounts, such as the *Greville Memoirs*, Cobbett's *Rural Rides*, Clarendon's *History of the Great Rebellion* and so on; there, harried by an accumulation of demands on his time, the personal researches of the student end, more or less at the point where the personal researches of the professional historian begin. The latter can delve in university libraries, in the British Museum, in the Public Records Office, and in public and private archives scattered about this and other countries, as he systematically examines unpublished, as well as published, material in a concentrated assessment of the history of a few years. The result may be an exact detailed study of great historical importance of the kind produced by Sir Lewis Namier and his colleagues on the early years of George III's reign. Depth to this degree cannot be even remotely matched by young historians dividing their time among several subjects and studying in outline the history of England and Europe, as most do, over a period of some two hundred years; even those who take the Special Subject paper find that in practice the resources and opportunities for first-hand study of sources are narrowly limited. Depth of knowledge and thought, since the two are necessarily closely related, is not likely to be found in the writing of the young historian. He cannot seriously hope to turn historical opinion upside down by some brilliant insight, based on profound research, into the military skill of Napoleon, for example, or the motives for Peter the Great's westernization policy in Russia, although these are examples of the type of subject on which he is expected to write in A Level, scholarship, and degree examinations.

It might be said that the student is equally at a disadvantage by comparison with the adult historian in using his width of knowledge to advantage. This is only partly true. The able young student has less knowledge at his command than the mature historian but he does not necessarily have less intelligence, and he may easily have more. Since intelligence consists of the ability to see connections of ideas the student may be able, just as readily as the senior historian, to see a similarity in character, for instance, between Gladstone and Luther, and there is no need for him to have read Gladstone's diaries and Luther's ninety-five theses first before he is fitted to make the comparison. Obviously he will not be able to make comparisons of this type from so wide a knowledge as that of the older historian; on the other hand, he may be able to see resemblances of character, or long-term causes or consequences of actions, which have escaped the notice of previous historians. He is much more likely to be able to show his originality and historical sense in this way than by a study in depth of little known documentary sources. The power to see resemblances of character, and the ability to put events in their historical context, sometimes over a very long period of history, are considerable merits in historical writing, and, as has been suggested, it is well within the capacity of the young student to make use of these methods to increase his effectiveness as a historian.

Seeing resemblances between historical events should not of course be carried to the stage where there is too much insistence on the exactness of the comparison. There are parallels, for example, between the restoration of the Stuarts in 1660 in England, and the restoration of the Bourbons in France in 1814. There are parallels between the invasions of Russia by Charles XII, Napoleon, and Hitler. Up to a point it is useful to draw attention to the fact mainly because, as each of these examples shows, there are certain recurrent motives and attitudes at work in history which seem timeless—the preference of nations for the safe mediocrity represented by the later Stuarts and Bourbons, for instance, after the turbulent excitements of Cromwellian or Napoleonic rule; or, in the second example, the heady influence of military success, and the inability of the powers of Europe either to make friends with Russia or to destroy her. In drawing attention to similarities of this kind, of character or event, the student, writing a brief essay, obviously only has time to do so by quick allusion rather than by detailed examination; but it is a habit of thought worth developing since it is one way in which he can widen his vision of history. When he gets to the stage where he can see in Disraeli something of the romantic opportunism of Sir Walter Raleigh, in T. E. Lawrence something of the ironic self-reliance of Sir Thomas More, then it does show in him a capacity to raise his head above the flood of detail and to see some of the more permanent qualities of mankind.

The occasions when cross-reference of this kind will occur will not be frequent but their value ought not to be forgotten. Width of approach is valuable in another way, more commonly found in historical writing, in the obligation on all historians deserving the name to put the events they describe in their right historical context. Events do not occur in isolation; policy decisions by rulers do not spring ready-made out of the skies; decisions, once taken, create a string of consequences which alter the course of later history. To write about the reforms of Peter the Great without mentioning the way in which many of his ideas had been anticipated by his predecessors, or to write about the 1848 revolutions without mentioning their relationship to the 1789 Revolution, is to show the writer's deficiency as a historian. Blindness to effects is as unintelligent as blindness to causes. Has France yet recovered from Napoleon, Britain from Queen Victoria, the United States from her Civil War, or the Far East from Vasco da Gama? These are far-reaching effects, and not always obvious, yet any young historian can train himself, or be trained, to see at least the immediate consequences of historic actions, whether he is writing about Lorenzo Valla's criticism of the Donation of Constantine, or the consequences for Sweden of the career of Gustavus Adolphus, or the dubious merits of the pseudo-settlement of Balkan problems made at the 1878 Congress of Berlin.

In international and, to some extent, in national history width of approach is also achieved by comparative assessment of the many similarities in policies which exist between country and country, especially in Europe. Metternich's comment that 'when France has a cold, Europe sneezes' is a recognition of the way in which national histories in Europe are closely related, and this has been so since the time of the Roman Empire. Amongst writers of European history the use of cross-reference becomes almost a reflex response. 'Austria,' writes I. Collins, 'entered the war nominally for the res- toration of the French monarchy, but by 1793 she was fighting, *like England* (my italics) for security.'[1] 'Unlike *Napoleon and Mussolini* (my italics) Hitler is devoid of the specific administrative gift,' wrote Fisher.[2] Books, such as those by M. S. Anderson[3] and H. Hearder,[4] which take this process a stage further and, ignoring national barriers, study administrative policies, and so on, as European phenomena, are particularly valuable in suggesting to Sixth Formers the possibility of escaping from the habit of studying each European country as if it were hermetically sealed off from the rest in its con- duct of internal and external affairs. The value of this international approach is certainly no less important in medieval history. Some of the examples are obvious—papal supremacy, monasticism, crusades, the special position claimed for the Holy Roman Emperor —and there are many more specific examples of identity of outlook amongst the European nations. There is, the striking similarity between Henry II of England and his contemporary, Philip Augustus of France, not only in their organizational energy but also in their concept of kingship, suggesting that the simultaneous development of monarchical authority in England and France did not come about solely by coincidence. Then, too, moving to later periods, how can anyone write effectively about the Reformation in England

[1] Op. cit., p. 92.
[2] Op. cit., p. 1206.
[3] *Europe in the Eighteenth Century 1713-1783* (Longmans, 1961).
[4] *Europe in the Nineteenth Century 1830-1880* (Longmans, 1966).

without mentioning Luther, Erasmus, and the influence of the New Learning in the Italian states and in northern Europe? Or, how can anyone write effectively about the reigns of Frederick II, Catherine II, or Joseph II, without mentioning those writers, French in name but European in outlook, Voltaire, Diderot, Rousseau, and the rest, who were trying to show rulers that they had an active responsibility to secure the welfare of their subjects? And could an assessment of Disraeli's foreign policy be adequate unless it were set against its European background of *Realpolitik* practised by Bismarck, Andrassy, and Gortchakov? Whether writing about national or international history one part of the mind needs always to be awake to the possibility of extending the issue being considered so that it is seen, at intervals, in its general context. In this way the young historian begins to develop the comparative sense which is part of the necessary outlook of any historian.

Concentration on the familiar themes of political, social, and economic history, is apt to lead students to underestimate the significance of artistic and literary achievement. They approach the arts with the unease of a junior curate invited to the bishop's palace. This is a pity. Painting, architecture, sculpture, and literature are original source material of first-rate importance. Documentary sources, drawn from public records, are more heavily weighted in favour of facts than feelings; they cannot generally match the power of the arts to capture the mood and spirit of an age. In trying to develop some width of approach the young historian ought not to close his mind to the opportunities which knowledge of artistic achievement can give, not only for its own sake but also, at times, for the light which it throws on political behaviour. Students, writing about Europe in the sixteenth century for instance, can readily see connections between the political realism of Henry VIII, or of Francis I, and the political realism of Machiavelli's 'The Prince'. They can learn a little about Henry VIII's qualities from the eye-witness description to be found in the letters and papers of the reign. 'He (Henry VIII) speaks French, English, Latin, and a little Italian; plays as well on the lute and harpsichord, sings from the book at sight, draws the bow with greater strength than any man in England, and jousts marvellously.' But students can add to their understanding of this useful quotation if they can link it with the background of Renaissance thought; for the great men of the Renaissance, versatility of the kind shown by Henry VIII came near to their ideal of *l'uomo universale*, the man of universal talents, able to attain excellence in whatever activity he undertook. This was the kind of versatility which Castiglione admired in *The Courtier*; when Henry's achievements are set in their context in this way then there is much more hope of understanding him and the age in which he lived.

The changes in outlook, so obviously present in the aftermath of the Renaissance, can be found almost equally easily in the artistic achievements of other periods. Yet, as the documentary sources of history become more voluminous when modern times are approached, the value of the arts in showing the hopes and fears of the succeeding generations can be increasingly overlooked. The result is the loss of any strong total sense of the period concerned, a weakness readily found in the works of specialist historians, though not among the more distinguished of them. By keeping his mind open to the possibility of showing the connection between the arts and other aspects of life the young historian can enliven and widen his approach. He may be able, occasionally, to see connections which have eluded the attention of senior historians. Pressure of time will limit his opportunities to develop these ideas at great length, but a few brief references will establish the fact that the writer does not study his subject with his nose for ever fixed to the grindstone of political history.

Examples of the way in which the works of artists strongly reflect the mood of their times are prolific. In writing about the causes of the French Revolution the young historian may well concentrate upon the scale of poor relief in the provinces of north-west France, and kindred economic and political matters; but if he is accustomed to placing events in a wide context he will not overlook the possibilities for comment on the outlook of the upper classes, which can be deduced from a study of the paintings of Watteau, Boucher, and Fragonard. Literary reference can be equally revealing. Wordsworth's ecstatic reaction to the French Revolution, the life of the English upper classes seen through the eyes of Thackeray in *Vanity Fair*, and of the lower classes seen through the eyes of Dickens in *Hard Times*, the disillusionment of twentieth-century intellectuals to be seen in T. S. Eliot's *The Waste Land*, these and countless other works of literature add at least a little to the vision of the historian. The quotation which follows shows how deftly knowledge of artistic achievement can be used to give depth to the concept of nationalism which, to the young writer, often seems to be a purely political idea.

The romantics became more firmly committed to nationalism as a new generation grew up which had not experienced the disenchantment of 1793. To the disciples of Byron and Shelley the French Revolution was a liberating fire whose flames should be carried to all the peoples of Europe. The role of the revolutionary was itself romanticized, the classic pictures which David had depicted giving way to ardent youths who fought with the workers in Delacroix's *Liberty on the Barricades* (1831).[5]

There are specialist historians who, whatever other admirable qualities they have, lack the insight to illustrate their knowledge with reference to the arts, but their work is the worse for it. It becomes further removed from shared human experience. It leads to the writing of what Sir Harold Nicolson sardonically described as 'many bright pages about pig-iron'. Yet there is no need for the specialist historian to be so limited in his outlook. Economic history and poetry, for instance, need not be for ever separated, like East and West, though the student who reads some of the writing on the subject might be forgiven for thinking so. Fortunately, there are some distinguished exceptions.

> Dash back that ocean with a pier,
> Strow yonder mountain flat,
> A railway there, a tunnel here
> Mix me this zone with that.

This verse from *Mechanophilus,* Tennyson's paeon to railways and seaside piers, would not find its way into an anthology of the best poetry, but as a means of showing the exhilaration of the Victorians over their increasing technical mastery is admirable.[6] This is the way in which the historian of wider vision finds evidence for his themes in sources which never occur to the historian of lesser ability.

Sometimes evidence from the arts may contradict evidence from other sources; if it does, so much the better. Problems in history

[5] I. Collins, *The Age of Progress* (Arnold, 1964), pp. 316-17.
[6] Professor C. H. Wilson, 'Economy and Society in Late Victorian Britain' (*Economic History Review,* 2nd Ser., Vol. XVIII, No. 1, 1965).

rarely have neat solutions, with all the evidence pointing with majestic certainty towards an unchallengeable verdict. If a new interpretation is solidly based, but clashes with conventional attitudes about the past, then it is the latter which need to be revised. The seventeenth century, for example, sandwiched between the Renaissance and the Age of Reason (as the eighteenth century is often described), is not a time in history when one expects to find in Italy, at least, the romantic mystical view of religion characteristic of the early Middle Ages. The people of the Italian states, one would have thought, had lived too close to disillusion for too long, to keep alive a sense of passionate devotion. Yet no one who studies Bernini's sculpture in *The Vision of the Cross*, or the superb design of the Piazza of St. Peter's itself, could doubt the force of religious feeling which they express. The quest for width of approach can thus be rewarding in suggesting a new line of thought, quite apart from its merits as part of the historical discipline.

The value of using allusive knowledge has been stressed because it is one of the ways in which the intelligent young historian can come very near to matching the skill of the senior historians; there is always the chance that he will become aware, while making comparisons of the kind suggested in this section, of a significant relationship which has been overlooked. He may then have the satisfaction of adding a little himself to the understanding of history; he becomes, if only temporarily, a pioneer, instead of following dutifully in the footsteps of his elders. Even if this can rarely happen his ability as a writer of history will be enhanced once he has understood that allusive knowledge, even if brief, is the product of a mind which has learned to study historical problems in their context.

The emphasis in this section has been upon those aspects of history whose value in illuminating a theme is easily overlooked. In addition, there are obvious opportunities for widening the approach to a theme by integrating the major branches of history—economic, political, social, and so on. This, however, is linked with the wider problem of collecting and analysing material, an important activity which justifies a section on its own.[7]

[7] See Section II, p. 65.

SECTION II

CONTENT

CONTENT

Knowledge of the means of expressing his ideas more sharply is an important addition to the skills of the young historian but it is obvious that literary skill alone is not enough. Nevertheless, students with some literary flair sometimes adopt an unwisely patronizing attitude to those other requirements of historical skill. A wide range of knowledge, accurate detail, and a recognition that, while objective judgement is perhaps impossible, the attempt to achieve it is crucial, these are obligations imposed on all historians of whatever standing. No amount of literary skill, however desirable in itself, compensates for the absence of these other qualities. They are the product of training as well as experience and the techniques described in the following sections will help the student in this respect. For the young historian involved, as most are, in preparing for examinations there are other requirements too. He needs, for instance, to be familiar not only with the types of question asked but also to have some understanding of the historical principles on which these questions are based. The section on question patterns has been written with this in mind. Examination questions of the traditional kind attract criticism, yet often they pose problems of historical understanding entirely appropriate for the abilities of the candidates. They are traditional not because of the inertia of examiners but because they perform their function more efficiently than any of the alternatives suggested, such as they are. The second special requirement for the young historian is that all his writing in examinations, and much of his writing in term-time, is conditioned by pressures of time to a degree which has no parallel in the work of senior historians. Within the space of 30-45 minutes the candidate has to be able to produce a relevant, concise, well-informed essay on a question which is, he hopes, familiar in subject-matter but which is unlikely to be familiar in wording. He has to be trained, therefore, for a specialized exercise and in the following sections his special needs have been kept strongly in mind. Some of the sections, notably that on topic analysis, are designed for reference rather than for continuous reading; they should be used as guides for the methodical preparation of material while that process is taking place.

1

TOPIC ANALYSIS

Sometimes questions are confined to particular aspects of policy, foreign, economic, administrative, and so on, but more often they are of a general nature in which a theme is set which needs to be confirmed or denied from as wide a range of evidence as possible. Accounting for the downfall of particular monarchs or countries, or, conversely, explaining their rise to power, discussing the causes of historical events, such as Parliament's victory in the Civil Wars, these and a host of other questions cannot be answered effectively without a wide review of evidence. This needs to be done systematically so that no branch of policy is overlooked. The scheme which follows is an attempt to show the student how this may be done. The questions suggested may sometimes yield no information; judicial change, for instance, may be non-existent during a given span of years; but each branch of policy needs at least to be considered, and some will need to be studied in detail.

The simplest division to make in studying policy is that between internal and external policies. Simple though this may seem, it is curious how frequently students in answering questions requiring a general assessment of a reign ignore one half or other of this basic division. This happens particularly, for instance, in analysing the reign of a ruler such as Charles XII of Sweden whose spectacular military activities in Europe can sometimes lead to total obliviousness of the damaging effects of those activities on the internal affairs of Sweden; conversely, the reforming policies of Joseph II, ranging from the ban on gingerbread making (as being harmful to the digestion of his subjects) to the abolition of serfdom, can divert attention totally from his much less striking activities in foreign affairs.

The failure to take into account internal or external policy as a whole is much less frequent, however, than the inability to distinguish between the different facets of these major branches of policy. By methodical analysis the whole range of internal and external policies can be examined; at the same time the student of history needs to be closely concerned with the motivations of policies, and with judgement of their effects and effectiveness; this aspect of his thinking is quite as important as the possession of an extensive narrative knowledge of a subject, and has consequently been given equal prominence in the analysis. A further preliminary comment which needs to be made is that the analytical method described assumes that the subject of study is primarily a reign or a ministry. There are, of course, many other topics studied in history, the various-isms, for instance, mercantilism, Enlightened Despotism, liberalism; then too there is the eminently sound view that European history ought to be grasped as an entity rather than be splintered into its component national parts, so that the absolutist tendencies of many of the European monarchies in the latter half of the seventeenth century, for example, can be set against the disorders of the first half, during which Russia experienced the Time of the Troubles, Britain experienced the Civil War, and major and minor powers in Europe engaged in the destructive Thirty Years War. Undoubtedly there is a gain in perspective and proportion if events in individual countries can thus be set in a wider context. The crucial point, however, is that intellectually this is a second stage operation. The general themes, absolutism and the like, have little meaning for the student until he has had a chance to study the particular evidence on which the generalizations are based. Furthermore, having studied the evidence, he is then in a position to assess to what extent the generalization is valid. Analysing the policies of individual rulers provides the first stage raw material on which the wider concepts of historical theory can be based. A study of mercantilism, for instance, involves some knowledge of theory but, unless this theory is firmly anchored to the facts of the economic policies of the various rulers alleged to be mercantilists, it is of little historical significance. Policy analysis thus provides the basic evidence which the student requires whether his problem is to assess the effectiveness of a particular ruler or of a particular policy, or even, as has been indicated, to test the validity of a general historical theory. Finally, the warning needs to be added for the over-zealous that the painstaking answering of every question mentioned below would take up far more time than most A Level candidates have available. The intention of the scheme is to suggest lines of thought which might otherwise be overlooked rather than to collect every particle of detail remorselessly.

1. Background influences

Rulers, however original and dynamic, cannot make all things new. They are conditioned by the activities of their predecessors, by the nation's geographical features, by its resources, by the prevailing mood of those who are influential in the nation's affairs, and by their own personal circumstances. Even such apparently dominant characters as Louis XIV, Peter the Great, and Napoleon, found that there were impersonal and personal barriers against which their power beat in vain. Historians speak of absolute rulers yet so often the term is a gross misnomer. Rulers are prisoners of history and are subject to conditioning influences which they can only partly overcome. In studying the activities of a particular ruler the first task is to be aware of those influences which modified and limited his policies. It is suggested that with this in mind the student should consider the following questions:

(a) *What are the physical characteristics of the country?*

This question, in turn, subdivides into several others:

Do the size of the country and its geographical characteristics hamper efficient central government?

Has it easily defensible frontiers?

Has it the natural harbours, great rivers, and general ease of communication to encourage trade?

Is the soil fertile?

Is the country well-stocked with mineral resources?

Has the country a large population, and is this population concentrated in a few large centres?

(b) *What historical circumstances have been influential upon the country?*

The first group of questions was concerned with the raw material of power. The second question centres upon the problems and opportunities arising from the use of those natural resources. It leads to these questions:

To what extent have the policies of the ruler's predecessors been advantageous to him? For instance, how efficient is the governmental system at central and local level?

How well developed is the country's economic power?

What improvements have been made in communications?

Is the financial system, e.g. banking, credit, taxation, government expenditure, working satisfactorily?

What are the relations between the central government and the various social groups, e.g. the Church, the nobility, the merchants, the professions, the masses in the towns and country, and in modern times, the various pressure groups?

Are the civilizing influences, e.g. the arts, scientific advance, education, making progress?

Are the country's armed forces well organized and powerful?

What are the national objectives in foreign policy and what progress has been made in attaining them?

Is the country a colonial power, and, if so, has this created any problems of policy?

(c) *What personal circumstances have influenced the outlook of the ruler?*
    The individual background of the ruler before he comes to power may often be significant, and should always be considered when trying to understand his behaviour when in power. Frederick the Great's policies, for instance, become much more intelligible once the student has knowledge of the methods of upbringing used by Frederick's father. The specific questions to consider are these:

What events and people are likely to have shaped the outlook of the ruler before he came to power?

What are the traits of character and ability which have emerged in the ruler in this preliminary period?

What trends of contemporary thought appear to have influenced his outlook?

2. Internal policies

(a) *What is the influence of the ruler upon the governmental system?*
   In assessing a ruler's policies early consideration needs to be given to the structure of government, and to his impact upon it. This is a relevant consideration whether one is assessing the attempts of Louis XIV, for instance, to strengthen central control in France, or of a modern British Prime Minister attempting to coordinate the miscellany of pressure groups seeking to influence policy. The student needs to be aware at this stage of the distinctions between executive, legislative, and judicial power. The Executive consists of the monarch and/or the chief minister, the cabinet or councils, ministers and civil servants, who are responsible for making policy and putting it into effect. Those officials responsible for implementing policy at local level are also part of the Executive. The Legislature is responsible for the wording of bills and may also have powers of scrutiny and control over the actions of the Executive. The Judiciary consists of the judges and magistrates who dispense justice in the courts. In a despotism all three divisions of government are controlled by the will of one man. At the other extreme democratic countries attempt, to some degree, to ensure that each main division of government has some independent authority of its own. In the United States, for instance, a written constitution ensures that the membership of the Executive, Legislative, and Judiciary shall be in separate hands, thus reducing the risk of one man, or group of men, being able to dominate the whole constitution.
   In judging the authority of a ruler or minister in a state it is clearly fundamental, therefore, to study the framework of government and to see how fully his control extends over its different branches. The general pattern of the governmental system will already be plain from studying the background influences at work, so that the main focus of attention will be upon the ways in which the ruler whose policies are being assessed modified this system.

This leads to the following detailed questions:

Who initiates policy? What part, for instance, is played by the ruler, by personal advisers, and by ministers? Are there any significant changes in this respect in the cabinet or conciliar system?

Are there any changes which affect government departments, e.g. an extension in their number, or modifications which affect the efficiency of the civil service?

Are any steps taken to improve coordination of central and local government activities?

Are there any developments affecting the powers and membership of the Legislature?

Are there any changes affecting the working of the courts?

To what extent is the Judiciary independent of the Executive?

(b) *Is there any increase in the nation's economic power?*

Economic activities may not be of such all consuming importance as Marxist historians assert but they are so clearly related to the material prosperity and military potential of a nation that they deserve close attention. These are the major questions to consider:

What considerations influence economic policy, such as war needs, or economic theories such as mercantilism?

Is active help given to agriculture and industry by, for instance, subsidies, loans, tariffs, technical education, and the encouragement of skilled immigrants?

Are communications improved?

Are natural resources increased by conquest?

What part is played by non-governmental agencies, for instance, guilds, trade-unions, banks, merchants, capitalists in the nation's economic activities? Are these activities modified by governmental legislation?

(c) *Is the financial system soundly organized?*

Students do not always grasp the distinction between economic and financial policies, but they need to do so. One revealing instance of the difference is the way in which France added substantially to her basic economic resources by overseas settlement and trading between 1661 and 1740 yet failed to take full advantage of these activities because of the inadequacy of her financial system. The difference is also apparent by comparison of the following questions with those in the previous section.

What problems arise in the collection of revenue, and to what extent and how are they overcome?

What sources of credit are available for the government and for individuals, for instance, industrialists? Is there sufficient credit available at low interest rates to encourage enterprise?

What are the objects of government expenditure, and are these objects wisely chosen?

(d) *Are there any changes in the size and efficiency of the armed forces?*

The size alone of the nation's armed forces gives an indication of its power. Efficiency and morale can compensate for a time for shortage of numbers, but in the long run, as the history of Sweden showed in the eighteenth century or of Nazi Germany in the twentieth century, victory usually lies with the big battalions. The point is that winning battles is only a part of the army's task; it then has the duty of garrisoning occupied territories or defending national frontiers: without substantial numbers these tasks cannot be fulfilled. The size of the armed forces also needs to be taken into account in assessing the strain on the country's economic and financial resources. Prussia's heavy concentration on armed strength in the eighteenth century, for instance, swallowed up revenue and labour at a rate which for many years gravely hampered industrial and agricultural development. The questions to ask are these:

What is the size of the respective branches of the armed forces during the period of rule being examined?

How successful are the armed forces in war? Are their training, morale, and leadership of a high standard? Do technical advances, for instance in weapons, or ship-design, strengthen the nation's military power? Are there any changes in the administrative system, such as the adoption of conscription, or the provision of supplies?

What other considerations influence the size and efficiency of the forces? For instance, there may be political or diplomatic reasons for maintaining a powerful army; alternatively, political or financial pressures may lead to reductions in the armed forces.

(e) *What influences do governmental social policies have upon the people of the country?*

Governmental policies towards the people are partly planned, partly improvised. Planning, for instance, may lead to systematic legislative attempts at social reform. On the other hand some policies have to be hastily improvised in face of a constitutional crisis perhaps, or of a war. The questions are these:

To what extent and by what means is the government able to establish a sound relationship between itself and the various social classes and group organizations within the community, for instance, the nobles, the churchmen, the middle classes, the masses in both town and country, the armed services, the professions, and the various pressure groups?

Are the various classes and groups satisfied with governmental policies, and, if not, how is their discontent shown?

Is the period marked, nationally, by notable intellectual and cultural advance. If so what part does the government play in this process?

3. *External policies*

These policies sub-divide into foreign and colonial policy. Sometimes these two policies are so closely inter-related that no useful distinction can be made between them. In both forms of activity it is desirable to see the motivations which are at work, and these will often be very similar as the questions show:

Is the motivation for external policies economic? Limitations in economic resources or a lack of good harbours may prompt aggressive external policies.

Is the motivation strategic, as in the desire to strengthen frontiers, or to maintain the balance of power, or in the formation of military alliances?

Is the motivation ideological? Is there a wish to impose a particular 'way of life' upon other nations?

Is the motivation influenced by the events of the recent past, such as the desire for a war of revenge?

Does the motivation spring primarily from a ruler's wish to make a strong impact upon the course of history?

Is the ruler's activity in external affairs dictated by pressure from individuals or groups within the state?

Actions are generally the product of an accumulation of motives but the questions above will help to disentangle the separate elements. Once this analysis has been completed the next phase is to examine the ruler's influence upon the course of events, and to see the consequences of his activities. The questions which arise are these:

What are the 'landmark' events—diplomatic activities, alliances, wars, and how are these related to the aims of the ruler?

What are the national, and international, consequences of the policy pursued?

How far are the activities of the ruler influenced by his skill and how far by chance events?

The process of acquiring colonial territories involves consideration of the same questions as those asked in relation to foreign policy, but there is an extension in that the student needs to consider these questions too:

What is the influence of the colonizing power upon the colonies in all the different phases of governmental activity, political, social, economic, and so on?

Are the relations between the colonies and the colonizing power amicable?

What are the advantages of the colonial possessions to the colonising power? Do the advantages outweigh the responsibility?

If all the questions listed under the three main headings of background influences, internal policies, and external policies, were answered, the information obtained would give a comprehensive basis for assessing the activities of a ruler or government. There may be occasions when a thorough assessment of this kind is needed. In general, however, the intention in suggesting this analytical scheme has been to indicate lines of enquiry for the student by showing him how to study a general topic by breaking it down into its main policy divisions and then into detailed questions. While it is unlikely that he will normally have the time to answer all the questions on all the branches of policy, awareness of what constitutes the main divisions of policy will widen his approach. The extent of probing he can do in answering the detailed questions under each main policy heading will obviously have to be varied in relation to the time available. Sometimes, however, the topic which he has been set will only involve one aspect of policy, such as foreign policy. In that event he will certainly need to collect information in answer to many or all of the questions listed under the main heading of foreign policy. It needs to be remembered though that policy decisions are often inter-related in a way which is not apparent at first sight, so that even if the student is confronted with a question on a ruler who pursued an adventurous foreign policy it is still instructive to have some knowledge of the course of internal affairs in his country, since these may be both influential upon his conduct of foreign policy, and be influenced by it. He would need in this instance not only to answer the foreign policy questions in detail, but also to scan the questions on the other branches of policy to see whether they suggest a relevant line of thought. Finally, whichever branch of policy is being examined the immediate and long term significance of the ruler's action, or inaction, needs to be given close consideration.

2

PREPARING AN ANSWER

Generally the student will be answering in essay form a question whose theme has been the subject matter broadly of a series of lessons. Note-taking, group discussions, and individual reading, are the main activities in which he is likely to have been engaged.

Students are usually diligent note-takers, but the accumulation of a mass of notes is not of significant value in itself. It may show industriousness of a mechanical kind, it may be an indication of the student's eagerness for knowledge, but the taking of notes may add very little indeed to the student's intellectual grasp of the subject. Even when the lesson is of high quality the mechanical operations of note-taking can reduce its value substantially. Sometimes the student does not know the teacher's plan of action; he cannot easily discern at first hearing the main sub-divisions of thought in the talk; he is hampered if he writes in long-hand by the patchiness of his notes, and by the loss of mental contact with the speaker as he engages in the processes of remembering what was said a minute ago, writing it down, and listening, if he can, to what the speaker is saying at the moment. The use of shorthand, conventional or unconventional, reduces these difficulties, though it does not remove them entirely. Whichever method is used it will be necessary for the student to give a substantial portion of his working time subsequently to selecting, organizing, and writing up the material likely to be of value. The amount of labour involved may be out of all proportion to the progress made.

One solution for these difficulties is for the teacher to issue typed notes on the subject-matter of the course. This saves much purely mechanical labour for the student and enables him to concentrate in lessons on the wider conceptual ideas which otherwise are apt to be swamped and confused in the process of scribbling down a mass of factual detail. Typed notes, issued in advance, also enable the student to see the structure of the talk, giving it an intellectual coherence which might not be clearly apparent otherwise to the industrious note-taker. If typed notes are not issued, and for a variety of reasons this will often be the case, how can the student make the best use of the material which he hears? He needs in the first place to realize the folly of trying to make a verbatim report of everything which is said. He needs to restrain his mind and his pen, and to be patient, until he is intellectually satisfied that the speaker has made a point of some significance. This means waiting until the speaker's train of thought on a particular aspect of the subject is concluded. A brief note to indicate the essence of the idea, and, where it is given, a source reference for further reading is then sufficient. This keeps to the minimum the time when the student is out of touch with the development of the speaker's ideas through absorption in the process of note-making. Generally it is possible, too, for the discriminating note-taker to catch up on the next main train of thought of the speaker before it has developed far enough to leave him mentally stranded. Note-taking of this kind leads to the collection of less bulky but more efficient notes, and has the further advantage of being more valuable intellectual training for the student than even the fullest verbatim report could ever be. A lecture, in brief, needs to be a fount of ideas, not a collection of facts which can be read in any text-book. Factual detail is important, but this kind of knowledge can be more intelligently acquired from the student's own reading of typed notes and books than from avid note-taking in lessons.

To this important subject of private reading a return will shortly be made but there is one other teaching device which is often considered to add to the student's grasp of the subject. This is group discussion. This method has won widespread support, partly no doubt as a reaction against the dullness which can easily arise in the traditional lecture form, partly, perhaps, because of the modern feeling that student participation ought to be encouraged and that the free atmosphere of discussion places students and the teacher on a more equal footing. On the other hand discussions do not provide the royal road for intellectual advance which is often assumed. They tend to be discursive and shallow if all the participants take part, a situation described by one cynic as 'a pooling of ignorance', or alternatively they differ little in practice from a lecture if they are dominated by the teacher or by one or two students. As a means of social training the discussion group can be useful if conducted by a sympathetic and intelligent chairman; as a means of helping the student to become a better historian its importance is over-rated. The individual tutorial is much more valuable in this respect, though ideally the student needs a tutorial at the planning stage of the essay as well as the traditional meeting for hearing the reading of his completed essay. In schools these planning tutorials can take place on a group basis, and are useful for discussing lines of approach, as long as the teacher avoids the trap of imposing a stereotyped version on his pupils.

However ingenious and efficient teaching techniques may be, they are all subordinate to the stage where the student, working on his own, begins to collect and organize his material to answer the essay set. Talks and discussions will have given him the outline and atmosphere of the subject, but it is his own reading which will give him the solid basis of evidence which he needs. For A level work, particularly, there is an abundance of modern text-books of high academic quality, and it is virtually certain that, whether the student is at school or attending a place of higher education, he will have available one or more thoroughly sound text-books. His first task in individual reading is to study the text-book account of the subject on which he is to write. It will be wasteful of his time if he makes notes as he reads. The policy to adopt is to read the whole of the relevant section and to note the page references of material which may be useful; more time-saving still is the practice of marking particular sections with a line and brief heading in the margin, though for the peace of mind of teachers and librarians students should confine this marking to books bought for personal use rather than books on loan. When the whole section has been read the student will then have enough grasp of the subject to be able to make an intelligent selection of material for his notes. Some of the points which at first reading looked as if they would be valuable often prove not to be so when the subject has been understood as a whole: the page references to them can then be discarded. The analytical system previously described (see page 65) will give the student a sound starting point from which he can explore in sufficient width and depth the question set. It will also suggest suitable headings and sub-headings. In making his notes the student will also be looking for useful and possibly striking comment by the author or by writers whom the author quotes himself.

The next stage is to strengthen this foundation of knowledge with some study of the work of specialist authors on the subject. Select bibliographies are frequently given in A Level history textbooks but provide little realistic guidance for the student unless accompanied by critical comment on the subject-matter and merits of the books listed. The advice of teachers or tutors is also essential at this stage if the student is to chart an intelligent course through the vast maze of printed words on history. In practice the A Level student will rarely have time for a study in depth of the specialist books. He may be able to look at one or two but even then his reading will not be of the painstaking kind which begins at page one and continues to the end. He will have to rely on selective reading, making use of the index and judicious skipping of narrative to concentrate in detail on short sections of the book. Relevance and striking or fresh expression of ideas will be the criteria to guide his reading, and the student will be well aware by this stage of the value of quoting from a well-known specialist authority.

The final stage of preparation consists of the study of original sources. This will often be a counsel of perfection for students coping with an accumulation of demands for essays, but the use of original sources is an essential part of historical study and the sooner the student acquires this training the better. The sources available to young students are mainly edited collections of documents, and this makes it unlikely that they will be able to startle the specialist historians with some explanation of past events never envisaged before. However, study of original sources has an intellectual value which is apt to be reflected in the student's essays, even if this amounts to no more than avoiding hackneyed extracts from documents. Rousseau's comment in *Du Contrat Social*, for instance that 'Man is born free but is everywhere in chains', is not the only phrase in that work which is worth quoting, and the student who is aware of that fact is beginning to show something of the outlook of the professional historian.

It could be argued that study of original sources should precede text-book and specialist book reading, and there may be times when this is true. On the other hand, the student needs to know the shape of the wood before he examines individual trees; some grasp of the general pattern of events is the first essential. However, whatever the order of reading, by the end of the period of preparation for an essay the student should have accumulated a number of ideas which, for convenience, are listed below.

1. A sound knowledge of the major 'landmark' events of the subject being studied, arranged, by means of notes or page references, either chronologically, or in policy groupings, or in ideas. The causes, effects, and significance, of each major event need to be understood.

2. Some knowledge of the characters of the rulers, ministers, or groups who influenced policy decisions, and of the characteristic intellectual outlook of the age being studied.

3. A number of interesting, relevant, and brief quotations with information about the source, and, where appropriate, the circumstances of each quotation.

4. An understanding of the appropriate technical terms used by historians in writing about the period concerned.

5. A strong grasp of the line of argument which will be followed in answering the question.

When this stage has been reached the student is almost ready to start writing his essay. From the moment the question was set the line of argument which he will follow has been taking shape in his mind, and each stage of the preparation will modify or confirm his first reactions. During the preparation therefore he will often be considering and evaluating evidence which does not fit in with the judgements he first formed, and this will lead to qualifications and even reversals of his preliminary ideas. But the crucial matter is that he should eventually reach a point where he can produce an essay which is consistent in argument, logical, and plainly dominated by the mind of the writer rather than by the minds of the authors he has read. He may very well make substantial use of the evidence provided by specialist historians, but a good history essay strikes an individual note of its own: it is more than a series of echoes of the writings of historians, however distinguished.

Once the writer has become clear about his approach to the question he can then begin to work out his paragraph organization, and to select an introduction. Some of the types of introduction frequently used by historians have already been examined;[1] whether the student uses one of these as a model, or one of his own devising, the essential points are that the introduction should be interesting in ideas, relevant, and well-expressed. Paragraph organization is a simpler matter, and the conventional advice given on the subject is adequate for the purpose. A paragraph should have a unity of its own; its subject-matter should be relevant to the question, and, if its relevance is not self-evident then the writer should give enough explanation to make it so; the first part of a paragraph should have a logical connection with the paragraph which precedes it, and the last part with the paragraph which follows it. As a matter of style paragraphs should not be too long since then they become boring and spoil the balance of the essay, nor too short because this produces a jerky incoherent effect in writing. In planning the paragraphs the headings alone are sufficient, so long as the student knows where, on paper or in his mind, he can find the appropriate subject-matter. The habit which some students have in examinations of writing out an elaborate essay plan before they start writing the essay itself is a great waste of time. It can be justified if the candidate feels very muddled about the question, or as an alternative to writing out a detailed answer if he is short of time, but neither of these situations is likely to arise if the candidate is a good one. In most circumstances, when a student has read and thought about his material, and has his argument clearly established in his mind, brief paragraph headings alone are sufficient to trigger off the information and ideas which the student has accumulated during the period of preparation. Finally, the conclusion, like any other leave-taking, ought to round off the occasion neatly and briefly. Logically the argument should be complete; stylistically the interest should be maintained right through to the final sentence.

[1] See pp. 37 ff.

3

QUESTION PATTERNS

Young historians, conscious of the difficulties of answering questions, are not likely to spare much thought for the difficulties of examiners in setting them.[1] Yet knowledge of the practical limitations which exist for examiners in testing the work of candidates of very mixed ability, whether in school or public examinations, can be instructive and possibly encouraging for the student. Many of the history papers set range over a very long period of time. The end of the fifteenth century is frequently taken as the dividing point between medieval and modern history, so that a paper on modern history, for instance, may cover the period from 1494 in European history, or 1485 in British[2] history, to at least 1939. The general practice is to concentrate on parts of these papers, so that the period studied will consist of some two hundred years, 1648-1848 in European history, or 1485-1688 perhaps in British history. Within this reduced period of study there are bound to be many movements and individuals of outstanding historical importance. The examiner in setting his questions may choose to ignore some but he cannot ignore all of these obvious topics since his aim is to set a fair test of the candidate's ability. Fortunately for the candidate's peace of mind, he is much more likely to be set a question on the influence of the possession of Hanover upon Britain's foreign policy in the eighteenth century than a question on the development of the Hanoverian pottery industry in the same period. The examiner is also limited in his question-setting by the types of candidates

[1] The opinions given here are based on personal observation. They do not represent the policy of any particular examining board.
[2] Welsh and Scots are understandably annoyed at times when, in spite of Acts of Union, and the careers of Livingstone, Lloyd George, and many others, the history of this period is blandly described as 'English' history.

examined. Since these include the mediocre border-line pass candidate as well as the future Oxbridge Fellow, a number of questions will be set which can fairly be described as conservative in subject-matter and in wording. The less able candidate who has worked diligently for two years needs to be given the opportunity of reaching pass standard and it would be a poorly set paper which failed to give him the chance of doing so. Most papers, however, include a few questions of a less obvious nature which the examiners hope will give the able candidate a chance to show his talents. This is not always so successful as is hoped since, from a combination of caution and shortage of time, the good examination candidate prefers to display his talents on subject-matter with which he, too, is thoroughly familiar.

The examiner also needs to ensure that the questions set are reasonably representative of the periods studied. In modern European history, for instance, the examiner will set a number of questions which are concerned with the highlights of the national histories of the major European powers. An examination paper which totally ignored the historical developments taking place in France, Prussia, Russia, and Austria, in the eighteenth century would be a very poor one. Sometimes, of course, the student's knowledge of these developments will be tested not by questions on a specific country, or ruler, but by questions requiring the student to link up his knowledge of the different countries; a question on mercantilism in the eighteenth century will test the student's knowledge of the economic policies of the major powers, and, preferably, of some of the minor ones too; questions on enlightened despotism, the role of the nobility in eighteenth-century government, the aptness of the phrases, 'The Age of Reason', and 'The balance of power', all these require answers which show the extent to which the student has detailed knowledge of events and attitudes in individual countries; they will also show how far he is capable of integrating his knowledge so that he is thinking in European as well as in national terms. The examiner, therefore, has some power of manoeuvre in this way over the type of question set; consequently the student needs to study European history both at the national and international level. If this sounds a daunting prospect he can take comfort from the fact that the questions set at both levels tend to follow well-worn tracks for reasons which have already been indicated. In British history the balance in question-setting which the examiner seeks is secured by seeing that each aspect of history, biographical, constitutional, military, economic, social, and cultural, is adequately represented.

It should be plain that the young historian's nightmare, in which he is confronted by a question paper filled with totally unfamiliar questions, is unlikely to materialize in reality. Most questions follow familiar patterns of thought, and it may be helpful to students, particularly those in Sixth Forms, to see some of the commoner approaches in question-setting set out clearly. Familiarity with the style of question set makes examination papers less formidable than they would otherwise be, and, apart from this, leads to greater efficiency in the preparation of material. There is frequent reference in the comments which follow to the need to base judgements on as wide a range of evidence as possible. Unless this is done systematically it is very easy even for a historian of some experience to overlook a relevant aspect of policy. The analytical method described in the previous section is helpful in eliminating this risk.

Question-setting cannot be reduced entirely to a few formulae but there is sufficient similarity between the questions set from year to year by the different examining bodies for some distinctive patterns to emerge; the examples which follow illustrate this point.

1. *Aims and extent of success*
At its simplest level this type of question appears in the form:

What were the aims of X (e.g. Metternich)? How far was he successful in achieving them?

Although the wording is humdrum and stereotyped, questions of this kind are more valuable in assessing the ability of different candidates than is apparent at first sight. If it is assumed for the moment that candidate A and candidate B write answers which are closely comparable in relevance, style, knowledge, and use of sources, what else remains to suggest that the historical ability of one is greater than that of the other? In brief the answer is width of approach. Any historical judgement which omits a major policy sector is obviously fallible; it is like trying to reach a verdict in the

court of law without having heard all the witnesses. The aims of X
are likely to have been numerous. He will have had aims in foreign
affairs and aims in home affairs. Each of these will subdivide further
still. In foreign policy X's attitude towards some powers may be
hostile, towards others friendly, so that his aims will not necessarily
be uniform. In home affairs he may have strong reformist aims in
his administrative policy combined with reactionary aims in his
treatment of the masses. He may have overriding philosophical or
personal aims which influence all aspects of his policy-making. His
aims may change even to the extent of complete reversal during his
period of power. The candidate who bears in mind these possibilities
is likely to write a better answer to the first part of the question
than the one who nonchalantly dismisses the complex aims of a
political leader in a few airy sentences.

The second half of the question is equally an exacting test of
historical judgement. The word 'successful'—and it is worth
stressing repeatedly the importance of probing the significance of
key words in a question—requires a verdict from the writer, even
if it is only the Scottish one of 'not proven'. Obviously, the verdict
will be more convincing if it is reached after a wide review of the
evidence collected from the different policy sectors, but in assessing
the success of a man's policies there are other considerations too.
He needs to be judged, for instance, in the context of his times not
those of the writer. The events which preceded the man's period
of dominance need to be known; so do the general assumptions in
thought and behaviour of his time; so do the impersonal factors
which condition policy, such as the geographical characteristics of
his country, its natural resources, the numbers, and racial com-
position perhaps, of its population. How would it be possible, for
instance, to arrive at a fair judgement of Metternich's achievements
without taking into account the volcanic effect of the French Revolution on European thought and politics, or without taking into
account the immense practical difficulties of governing the sprawling
Habsburg Empire and of attempting to preserve the Vienna settlement in Europe. Nor could Metternich always have his own way.
The Emperor could be recalcitrant, and after 1835 the obstruction-
ism of Court circles to Metternich's policies became a major
obstacle to his plans. Knowledge of the specific limitations of time,
place, and circumstance, is thus clearly of paramount importance

in arriving at a considered judgement of a man's political career. Although the 'aims and extent of success' type of question may seem unimaginative it has the salient virtue of testing the candidate's historical powers quite searchingly, as has been shown, hence the frequency with which it appears on examination papers. So long as the candidate has grasped the implications just described of the question, answering it should present no great difficulties, though a good answer requires widely based knowledge and a sound historical sense.

Questions based on the 'aims and extent of success' approach frequently appear in faintly disguised form as quotations on which comment is invited. The similarity of pattern is apparent in these characteristic examples:

Is Joseph II's self-judgement that he failed in everything he undertook justified?

'An ill-deserved reputation for greatness.' Consider this assessment of *Catherine II.*

'The ablest politician of her reign'. Discuss this judgement of *Elizabeth I.*

'A fruitless search for glory abroad and stability at home'. Discuss this comment on the policy of *Napoleon III.*

Questions of this kind are prolific. The approach to them does not differ significantly from that described in the more simply worded question on the 'aims and extent of success of X'. As with all questions the candidate must focus strongly on the key word or words of the question. In the question on Catherine II, for instance, the evidence which the writer supplies must point to the theme of greatness with the fixed certainty of a compass needle pointing to the north. Definition, or at least further clarification of the crucial words in these questions, is vital. One cannot write effectively about 'greatness' or 'political ability' or 'a fruitless search' and so on, without a very clear understanding, conveyed equally clearly to the reader, of the precise meaning to be attached to these terms. Failure to do this produces the vague answer of uncertain relevance common amongst the weaker candidates. An equally common failing amongst weaker candidates is the inability to see that many of these questions are, to use examiners' jargon, 'open-ended'. Rulers die but their policies outlive them. Joseph II was depressed by the apparent failure of his reign in 1790, the year of his death. Might he have been less gloomy if he had been able to foresee, as the historian knows, that the revolutionaries of 1848 would place a wreath on his statue? Clumsy, dictatorial, obstinate, he intended in his own odd way to liberalize the Empire and 'to make his people happy'; these were intentions of more permanent value and possibly of greater historical significance than the power politics of Frederick II or Catherine II whose activities seem so much more successful, and it was this which the 1848 revolutionaries discerned. The historian with a knowledge of the events of the nineteenth and twentieth centuries is better equipped than Joseph himself to judge his success. Recognition of this advantage is one mark of the abler candidate. In making his judgements he takes into account long-term effects of policies extending possibly long after the death of the ruler or statesman who initiated them.

2. *Historical context*

A sense of historical continuity ought to be one of the by-products of historical training. The 'open-ended' question tests this capacity; so too, do those questions which specifically set characters in the context of their national histories and ask for an evaluation of their importance. These examples demonstrate the approach:

How far did X (e.g. Bismarck, Louis XIV) change the course of his nation's history?

Was X (e.g. Frederick William the Great Elector, Henry VII, Peter I) the founder of his nation?

These questions and others like them, such as 'Assess the contribution to the Church of England of William Laud', make it imperative that the candidate should deal with the question in three phases. The state of the country or institution before the impact of the central character was felt has to be described; the immediate effects of his policy are next studied, and finally the long-term effects.

Neglect of any one of these phases fundamentally weakens an answer; so too does a narrative recital of policy decisions unrelated to the theme of national change.

3. *Single Policy*

The characteristic of the question patterns studied so far have been the insistence on width of approach. The converse is the need to induce candidates to probe particular branches of policy in depth. In a minor way the student is then able to see some of the problems of historical research of the kind illustrated so well for instance in Sir Lewis Namier's painstaking analysis of the 1761 Parliament. Some students respond more readily to the historical context type of question giving scope for the eagle's eye view of history of the kind to be found in the writings of Trevelyan and H. A. L. Fisher; others prefer microscopic exactitude of detail, and the single policy question may suit their talents. These are some typical examples:

How tolerant had Englishmen become in religious matters by 1714?

What was the basis of Napoleon's military success?

Was Louis XIV's foreign policy more personal than patriotic?

Most A Level candidates, except in the Special Subject papers, are studying European and British History in outline only, consequently the amount of detailed knowledge they can provide in a specialized policy question is necessarily limited. Nevertheless there are certain themes of a conspicuously obvious kind, such as Napoleon's military ability, which can fairly be set and which do require some power of detailed analysis and critical judgement. Knowledge of detail is plainly the paramount factor in questions of this kind, and the risk of irrelevance is reduced by the specific wording of the question. Even though there will be a heavy concentration of attention on the particular aspect of policy asked, it is still worthwhile for the student to remember that the different branches of policy are not conducted in watertight compartments. A narrowly based answer to the question on Napoleon's military success might concentrate, very competently, on the brilliance, mobility, and superb timing of Napoleon's manoeuvres at Ulm, at

Austerlitz, and in Italy, answering the question in terms of Napoleon as a battlefield leader. This might make a very good answer to a part of the question. What it would lack would be the breadth of historical understanding which would demonstrate to the reader the debt Napoleon owed to the military reforms of the pre-Revolutionary period, to the Revolutionary spirit itself, to chance, to the weakness of his opponents, and to the administrative and economic developments which provided him with war materials and troops. An all-round approach is a much more illuminating answer to questions of this kind than one which confines itself in this instance to Napoleon's military manoeuvres.

4. Comparisons

Among the various types of question asked on individual histori-cal characters one of the most familiar is that which requires the student to recognize the similarities and differences between two characters. These questions provide a good test of the writer's sense of relevance and of his powers of analysis. The choice of characters is almost limitless.

Compare and contrast the elder and younger Pitt as war leaders.

Compare and contrast the attitudes of Anselm and Becket towards their responsibilities as Archbishops of Canterbury.

Compare Catherine II and Joseph II as benevolent despots'.

A common weakness in answer to these questions is to write an answer consisting of two distinct parts. One part contains an account of the activities of character A, and the other an account of the activities of character B without any attempt whatsoever to show any connection, whether of resemblance or difference, between the two. Establishing this connection persistently is one characteristic of a good answer: another is to give far more attention to the ideas and influence of the characters concerned than to the narratives of their lives. Answers ought not to consist of extended versions of the kind of entry one finds in the Dictionary of National Biography.

The need to establish clear connections between the component ideas of the question applies equally strongly, of course, if the question is concerned with movements rather than men. Questions such as:

Why was Sweden less powerful in the eighteenth than in the seventeenth century?

Discuss the differing characteristics of Lutheranism and Calvinism.

illustrate this point.

5. *National development*

Assessment of national progress or decline provides a means of testing whether the candidate is capable of putting into a wider context the activities of a series of rulers, and also whether he is aware of the impersonal factors which, in part, govern a nation's history; these are often more evident over a longer tract of time than they are within the narrower limits of a reign. Although the wording of the following questions does not at first sight appear to have much in common each one is broadly concerned with the same issue, the strengths and weaknesses of the countries concerned.

'Swedish power and influence in the seventeenth century were not strongly rooted'. Discuss.

Why was Poland partitioned in the eighteenth century but not Turkey?

Why was the unification of Italy in the nineteenth century so long delayed?

The internal conditions of the countries mentioned are plainly relevant and a substantial part of the answers would have to be given to the governmental system, economic position, and the various other factors described in the section on topic analysis. But this information will only partly answer questions of this type. External policies will also have to be examined and this will involve knowledge too of the external policies pursued by neighbouring countries. In eighteenth-century Poland, for instance, the power of that country to develop any independent external policy (or internal policy for that matter) was negligible. Consequently the question on Poland would involve assessment of the foreign policies of Prussia, Russia, and Austria, in relation to Poland, rather than of any individual diplomatic or military initiative by that country itself. On the other hand, the question on Sweden involves a rather different emphasis in that until the end of the seventeenth century the political initiative in Sweden rested strongly with Sweden herself; even so the growing strength of Russia and Prussia would have to be taken into account as a long-term explanation of Sweden's decline.

6. *'Label' terms*

'Label' terms such as the three field system, the Renaissance, Enlightened Despotism, mercantilism, Agricultural Revolution, liberalism, nationalism, and so on, are convenient in the writing of history as a means of referring to general trends in governmental practice or in social and economic development; their historical convenience is plain from the fact that very frequently these terms were not used by those who lived in the period concerned but have been invented subsequently by historians. The term 'Industrial Revolution' for instance was not used until 1837, when Blanqui so described it, and it was not widely adopted until Arnold Toynbee's *Lecture on the Industrial Revolution of the Eighteenth Century in England* published in 1884. Adult historians are very well aware, or should be, that terms of this kind are only generalized descriptions, and that they can be challenged in detail. The young historian, however, not long past the stage where history consisted for him of making simple factual statements on matters such as the sequence of events during the Spanish Armada finds himself confronted in books with these 'label' terms, expressed sometimes as if they had the same objective value as the statement that Henry VIII had six wives. Part of historical training consists of recognizing the difference between facts, which can be accepted at their face value, and opinions which, whether they come from contemporaries of the event or from historians, have to be scrutinized very carefully. Questions on 'label' terms are a useful means of testing whether the student has developed critical historical judgement. As examples, questions on 'absolute monarchy' in the middle ages, on 'nationalism' in the nineteenth century, or on 'socialism' in the twentieth, give ample opportunity to the student to examine these terms closely, and to show the loose thinking which often accompanies their use. Having made it clear that he recognizes that these terms are only a rather inadequate form of historical shorthand to represent general tendencies in behaviour, in which the exception is almost as frequent as the rule, the student can go on to trace their influence in the particular context which the question requires. Since historians themselves in specialist books and articles plough and replough the ground again and again in assessing these 'label' terms at what they believe to be their true worth, the student who keeps himself in touch with trends in historical thinking has a distinct advantage. This does not mean that his essay should be entirely dominated by the names and opinions of prominent historians. It is his work which is being examined not theirs, and his own judgement on the issues ought to be conspicuously present. The following examples show specifically how questions on historical movements may sometimes be phrased.

What do you understand by Enlightened Despotism? Do you agree that the rulers of eighteenth century Europe were more apt to be despotic than enlightened?

Why did Liberalism make so little headway in Europe in the first half of the nineteenth century?

'Evolution rather than revolution'. Discuss this view of the changes taking place in industry in Britain in the second half of the eighteenth century.

Discuss the influence of Feudalism upon the structure of society in Norman England.

7. Cause-effect

Much of history consists of studying cause-effect relationships and this emphasis is frequently shown directly in examination questions. The question may be simple, sometimes deceptively simple, in its wording. For instance,

Why was there a French Revolution?

To show an awareness of the major influences at work, to give each one its due share of attention and no more, and to do so within the space of the forty minutes or so available to examination candidates on each question, is an intellectual feat of some merit requiring knowledge, judgement, and quick thinking. Often the question may appear less all-embracing than the example just given yet, on reflection, may demand an equal width of approach. Questions, for instance, which ask whether the French Revolution was the product of social and economic circumstances, or whether it was the result of the deficiencies of character of Louis XV and Louis XVI, necessarily involve a wide review of other possible causes if they are to be answered sensibly. The cause-effect approach lends itself particularly to the type of question in which the examiner sets up an Aunt Sally in the hope that the candidate will have enough confidence in his own judgement to be able to knock it down. The question might be phrased like this:

'The peace-makers at Versailles were making war not peace.'
Discuss.

The weakness of the Versailles peace settlement would need to be considered; at the same time the candidate would need to show an awareness that there were other influences at work, some of them having little or no connection with the Versailles settlement, in the events leading up to the 1939-45 war. The essential difference between the answers of a good and a poor candidate to questions of this type is that the latter often does not range widely enough in his ideas. Historical events are produced by a multiplicity of causes, and it does not help to narrow the choice down too drastically. Nor does it reflect any credit on the student's training in history if he accepts every statement at its face-value.

Study of causation opens the way to a vast array of questions in which the influence of particular men is studied.

What were the contributions of Clive and Warren Hastings to the extension of British power in India?

What was the influence of Colbert upon the growth of power of the French monarchy?

What was the influence of Bentham upon nineteenth century methods of administration?

What was the influence of Bismarck's foreign policy on international relations either before or after 1870?

Relevance, as in any other type of essay which basically involves two component ideas, is easily lost by dealing with each idea as if it were totally distinct from the other. In the question on Colbert, for instance, an answer which described first Colbert's activities and then, secondly, the growth in power of the French monarchy, without explicitly establishing any connections between the two ideas, is plainly unsatisfactory; yet, when the young historian becomes absorbed in the detail of his answer, he easily makes this kind of mistake. He may be able to see the connections in his own mind, but he needs to realize that it is not good enough to leave the reader to work out the relevance of the writer's ideas by means of telepathy.

The tendency of modern historians to pay rather more attention to movements and rather less to men sometimes leads now, especially in post A Level examinations, to a simple reversal of the type of question which asks the candidate to trace the influence of a man upon the course of affairs. After some of the recent historical assessments of Bismarck's foreign policy, for instance, it might be more appropriate to ask 'What was the influence of international relations upon Bismarck's foreign policy?' rather than the reverse.

The cause-effect relationship lends itself admirably to the purpose of finding out whether the candidate is able to connect the past and present in an intelligent way. It does not require great historical knowledge or ingenuity, for instance, to see the ways in which the outlook of European and other nations has been modified by the Renaissance and the Reformation, the French Revolution and the Industrial Revolution, right up to the present day. The student with any claims to historical ability ought to be able to see the long-term significance of events in this way. Historical subjects ought not to be studied as if they existed in sealed-off compartments. A question about the causes of the Civil War in England, for instance, cannot be answered solely in terms of the quarrels between Charles I and Parliament. The mid-seventeenth century outburst of violence was partly the product of the policies and attitudes of James I also; it was also the product of the changing role of Parliament under the Tudors. Similarly, questions phrased in the following way require a good grasp of long-term influences in history.

Were X's (e.g. Henry VI) problems inherited or of his own making?

The examples given indicate some of the more common
approaches found in question-setting. Other variations are possible
but enough have been given to suggest ways in which the young
historian can usefully think about the material which he is studying. Examining causes, describing events, and tracing consequences,
provide basically the subject-matter of history, and the questions
reflect these different aspects of historical thinking.

4

JUDGEMENT

Judgement requires a judge, and this is how the young historian should think of himself. The judge hears the prosecution and the defence, then sums up for the benefit of the jury: so, in effect, does the historian. Like a judge, the historian needs a strong sense of relevance, a scrupulous care over the meaning of words, a critical approach towards evidence, and a willingness to give due weight, but no more, to expert opinion. Unlike a judge in a jury case, the historian has to reach a verdict (even if it is only the cautious Scottish one of 'Not proven') as well as to present the issues; finally, while judges may be able to combine a very great reputation with a very dull manner, this ought not to be the ambition of the young historian: he has the writer's obligation to be interesting as well as instructive. In using his judgement on a historical problem three matters deserve particularly close study by the student—relevance, the validity of evidence, and the soundness of his own comments.

1. *Relevance*

When Dr. Johnson was asked which was the greatest virtue he said that courage was, 'since without it there would be no security for any other'. Precisely the same comment would apply to relevance if a choice had to be made of the most important quality in writing. Literary skill and extensive knowledge are worthless unless an essay keeps to the point; and it must keep to the point in every paragraph. In so short a piece of writing as an essay where ideas have to be developed rapidly it ought to be possible for the writer or reader to be able to isolate any paragraph from the essay and for him to be left in no doubt at all of its relevance to the question set. Often the writer takes the trouble to make the relevance of each paragraph explicitly clear. If, for instance, a question were set on Peter the Great's claims to be a reforming genius, the writer might very well take as his central theme the idea that many of Peter's reforms had been anticipated by his predecessors. One paragraph might be given to changes made in the government of the Church by Peter, followed by mention of the stormy relations of Church and State in the mid-seventeenth century culminating in the victory of the State when the Tsar Alexis banished the Patriarch Nikon to a remote northern monastery. If the writer, having stated the facts in detail, concludes the paragraph by saying 'As in so many of Peter's reforms his changes in church organization merely gave new force to attitudes which had long existed in Russia; in this sense Peter was no reformer', then the reader is left in no doubt whatsoever about the relevance of the paragraph.

Examiners and teachers, marking many scripts, are not ungrateful when the candidate firmly directs their minds in this way to the relevance of his arguments. If he does so in every paragraph so much the better. It need not be done in a monotonous way. The sentence establishing relevance can come at the beginning of the paragraph sometimes instead of at the end; in addition, the writer can vary its phrasing to avoid a monotonous formula of words, though even that is better than leaving the reader bewildered as he tries to puzzle out the connection between the paragraph and the main theme. Sometimes a writer can develop so much impetus in his argument that the relevance of individual paragraphs is self-evident, but a writer would have to be very optimistic to imagine that this is always possible. It is not merely a matter of the writer's skill in argument. Certainly the young historian should not feel that it is a weakness in his ability to develop an argument if he makes the relevance of his ideas explicitly clear. The wording of the question, an original approach by the writer, and consideration for his reader, may all at different times influence a writer, quite justifiably, to use key sentences as signposts for the reader's benefit along the route of the argument. This is a source of strength not weakness in writing; it removes uncertainty in the mind of the reader following the argument, and it clarifies the writer's approach in his own mind too. It could be added with equal truth that not only every paragraph but even every sentence in an essay should be relevant, either on its own or else as a necessary preliminary in leading to an idea which is directly relevant.

Irrelevance is the greatest single cause of poor work and of the poor marks that go with it, yet, once the young historian learns how to use every paragraph as a hammer-blow upon the theme of the question, the art of doing so is unlikely to desert him afterwards. Like driving, the skill once acquired becomes largely automatic. In hammering home an argument it will generally be necessary to return again and again to key words or phrases in the question. Terms may have to be defined. No writer could make much headway with questions involving 'Enlightened Despotism', 'mercantilism' 'liberalism in the nineteenth century', and so on, without making clear the exact meaning he attaches to those terms. If these semi-technical terms of history provide the main theme of the question, as they often do, then they should occur many times in the answer. Whether the writer decides for instance, that Catherine II was 'an enlightened despot', or not, these words should appear as frequently in his essay as 'King Charles' head' appeared in the writing of David Copperfield's Uncle Dick, only one hopes with more relevance. Repetition of the wording of the question may be equally necessary of course if no technical term is involved. If the question were asked, 'Economic distress was not a major cause of the French Revolution. Discuss.', then there are three concepts in the question on which to focus the mind—'economic distress, 'major cause', 'French Revolution'. Historians have shown how the French Revolution came in a series of well-defined stages between 1787 and 1789 and perhaps one should more accurately speak of the French Revolutions of those years. This verges on pedantry, but examination of the term 'French Revolution' would make a relevant section of the essay since it could be shown that different groups of the community had different aims, and that economic distress was certainly not a cause of the defiance of King Louis XVI by the Assembly of Notables in 1787, nor was it primarily a cause of the plottings of the middle class Revolutionary leaders in Paris. The words 'economic distress' obviously involve examination of the extent to which that description was true, and the provision of evidence on the scale of poor relief in different parts of France, the standard of farming, the influence of bad harvests on living conditions in town and country, and so on. Finally, what justification is there for considering 'economic distress' to be 'the major cause' of the French Revolution? Clearly this involves examination of other major causes too—the frustration of the middle classes, the qualities of the French Kings after Louis XIV, the system of government, the wars in which France was involved in the eighteenth century, and the growth of a spirit of critical enquiry in spite of attempts to suppress it.

The point is, therefore, that in every question set there are key phrases which require the closest scrutiny. Nothing in the question should be accepted unthinkingly. As was mentioned, even so familiar a concept as the French Revolution which is generally taken for granted as a simple statement of fact, becomes more complex when the events which compose it are closely analysed. The mediocre candidate betrays his weakness by failing to examine sufficiently intensively the wording of the question. He agrees too readily with what is put in front of him whereas the stronger candidate is capable of breaking down a question into component parts, with some of which he may agree, with some of which he may disagree. He may feel sometimes, particularly perhaps in a question which involves discussion of a quotation, that the view expressed in the quotation is altogether too narrow in approach to be satisfactory as a statement. Suppose, for instance, that the question consisted of the quotation ' "Britain in 1900 was at the zenith of her power and influence." Discuss.' The writer might briefly concede that in some respects, such as her naval power, Britain was at the zenith of her power and influence in 1900, but he might very well devote the rest of his essay to showing that the quotation is a gross over-statement. The words 'In 1900' might arouse his comparative historical sense, and he could with advantage to his argument consider whether it might not be fairly claimed that Britain in earlier times was much more strongly placed, as she was in 1763 for instance. The bulk of his essay, presumably, would be devoted to showing the weaknesses developing by 1900 in Britain's economic, military, and international position. Refusal in this way to allow the wording of the question to dictate his ideas is a mark of the stronger candidate though he must be able to substantiate his arguments and he must be relevant.

Writers of this kind are far removed from those students who treat every question as if it began with the words 'Give an account of ...' Narrative is bound to be used in some parts of the essay but it is subsidiary to analysis. Perhaps the most useful guide to the young historian is for him to look upon an essay as an argument during which he has to establish his line of approach firmly, interestingly, and in a short space of time, as he would have to do in a debate. If he develops his ideas at the leisurely tempo which is possible in writing a book, he will never make a good essay writer. After O Level the young historian is unlikely to encounter any question which has to be answered purely in terms of narrative; the sooner, therefore, that he frees himself of this approach the better. Presumably he does not want to think of himself as an Ancient Mariner, waylaying a reluctant audience, and reciting an endless stream of largely irrelevant facts, but this is, in practice, a common weakness in the work of Sixth Formers as they make the transition from O Level to A Level work. Once this transition has been achieved it represents a great gain in ability and confidence in the subject. After two or three years in the Sixth Form the student is often capable of writing lively, relevant, and well-informed answers which might well be little inferior to those which experienced historians, writing in the same conditions, could produce.

2. *Evidence and comment*

If evidence is to be convincing it needs to come from a reliable source, and it needs to be precise. In schools the sources of information are teachers, books, and to a lesser extent, specialist journals, memoirs and edited collections of documents. In further education the balance changes a little so that more attention is paid to specialist books, and articles and documentary sources are studied in greater depth. There are certain sectors of historical study where evidence can be accepted from a text-book just as confidently as it can be from an original source. There is no need, for instance, to examine a full copy of the original version of the Treaty of Vienna in order to state that its terms were finally settled in 1815; and although historians, in stating the terms, make a selection of what they consider to be the most important clauses, and disagreement is possible with them over their choice, few students have the time until the post-graduate stage to examine objectively every fact or selection of facts with which senior historians confront them. The

Sixth Former and, to a greater extent, the undergraduate can do a certain amount of this personal verification of factual statements made in books, but time, if nothing else, prevents them from doing so consistently; this is regrettable since it is an important part of historical training, but so long as the main aim of examiners is to test outline knowledge of long periods of time detailed personal research is scarcely practicable. Factual knowledge therefore has generally to be taken on trust by the student. His chief responsibility in this respect is not to counter-check every fact but to ensure that his knowledge is as precise and detailed as possible. Ignorance of detail cannot for long be concealed; the candidate who produces one generalization after another without supporting evidence may sometimes feel that he is being brilliant but it is a feeling unlikely to be widely shared. The contrast between a loose and an exact style of writing is shown in these two examples:

1. 'Russia could not develop trade with the west on a large scale because she lacked ports. Peter was able to improve this situation, however, when, as a result of the fighting against Sweden, Russia made a favourable treaty which gave her outlets to the Baltic. In addition, the making of St. Petersburg gave another outlet to the Baltic, and consequently trade with the west greatly increased.'

This extract shows that the writer has a general grasp of this aspect of Peter's policies, and the ideas are developed logically; but it glosses over detail and is less convincing than the following extract on the same theme.

2. 'In the early years of Peter's reign the chief port for trading with the west was Archangel, ice-bound for half the year. Yet, between 1690 and 1725, the year of Peter's death, there was a tenfold increase in the number of western ships trading with Russia. Peter's initiative in founding St. Petersburg in 1703 partly explains this change; but equally important were the two ports of Riga and Reval, allocated to Russia by the terms of the Treaty of Nystadt in 1721, following the long war which destroyed Sweden's Baltic empire.'

The greater precision of the second example gives it more impact, and illustrates the value of close observation of detail in reading. The sentences are well packed with exact geographical, historical, and statistical information, all clearly related to a single theme. Dates are given, not for their own sake, but as a reminder of Peter's persistence throughout his reign in developing trade with the west. One warning, however, needs to be given in examining the importance of factual information. Students, rightly aware of the uselessness of a vague answer, sometimes go to the opposite extreme and cram their answers indiscriminately with factual information. The point is that facts need to be used in support of ideas not as a substitute for them.

If history consisted simply of accumulating factual evidence of a simple kind, listing treaty terms, describing legislation, tracing the course of wars, and so on, the demands on the historical judgement of the student would be trivial. Much more is involved. Often questions are asked which are matters of opinion not of fact. 'Did the Glorious Revolution change the course of British History?' 'Was Napoleon a benevolent despot?'. Questions of this kind cannot be answered as if they were geometry theorems. Confronted with the words, so popular with the examiners, 'Discuss', 'Estimate', 'Assess', 'Compare', the student has to try to avoid the pitfalls of prejudice, his own and other people's. In practice this can never be fully achieved. Each writer of history has his own individual approach, coloured by his own experience and personality. He may have a stronger interest in one branch of history, economic, constitutional, or whatever else, than in any other. He may be an admirer of dictatorship or he may believe that liberalism is ultimately the universal answer to the problems of government. He may have overmuch sympathy for characters in history whose personalities happen to resemble his own, or he may have too little sympathy for those whose characteristics resemble too closely those he dislikes in his own colleagues. Personal prejudices are endless and are just as likely to be found in primary sources as in modern books. How far, for instance, can one accept the memoirs of Napoleon, of Bismarck, or of Clarendon, as faithful accounts of the events with which they were connected? Even Thucydides, who goes to great pains to point out his reliance on first-hand sources, cannot prevent his personal admiration for Athens breaking through to the surface of his writing. When one comes to modern times how far can the student be sure that the book he is studying is free of the vanity of the scholar anxious to show that his predecessors and fellow-scholars have all been following a false trail? Supposing it were possible to create the perfect historian, free of personal animosities.

vanities, and peculiarities, devoid of fanaticism for this or that cause, thoroughly trained in the assessment of evidence, how far would he be able to understand the motivation for events, and how far could he accurately trace their full effects? The idea cherished by historians, such as Lord Acton at the turn of the century, that it was only necessary to be patient, and that, then, history, grown scientific and specialized under the influence of the German school of historians, would one day be fully known, was and is a delusion. Scholars may spend a lifetime examining documentary sources, academics may argue, lecture, and write, but a full understanding of why men acted as they did, and what the full effects of their actions were will elude them all.

The point is that the evidence which the past has left is incomplete, as well as being unreliable. It is like trying to complete a jig-saw puzzle with half the pieces missing. History is not bunk, in spite of Henry Ford, but it can be a sham when it claims to depict the past with an accuracy which is in practice, beyond human grasp. If the great men of the past have the opportunity, wherever they are now, of seeing their own biographies, and the learned criticisms of them, they must often feel a mixture of indignation and amusement which would be enlightening to see. Motives, for instance, remain obscure because they were seldom committed to paper, and, if they were, are not always to be believed any more than a diary is when a writer suspects that it will become public knowledge. No one knows in full, for example, why Frederick II attacked Silesia in 1740. Simple explanations can be given: Prussia's economic needs, the need to strike first before the other powers did so, the relative strengths and weaknesses of Prussia and Austria in 1740, the prevailing standards of political morality, and many other reasons reflecting the ingenuity of the writers. What is missing from this elaborate facade is the keystone itself, the personal motivation which, somewhere in the recesses of Frederick's mind, made all these elements and others unknown to us fuse together so that at a given moment in time he took the decision to attack Silesia. Historians can describe some of the elements in the situation; they cannot describe them all. What is true of the one episode described can be applied with equal force to others. Why did James II behave with such wilful blindness to the consequences? Why did George III conduct relations with the American colonies in the way he did? Why did Napoleon engage in the ruinous Moscow campaign? Research and painstaking analysis will not provide all the answers. What has to be realized is that there are great sectors of human life and thought in the past about which nothing is known and nothing, in human terms, ever will be known.

Scholars sometimes affect to despise what they describe as 'psychological' history. If they are thinking in terms of wild guessing at motivation as a substitute for the examination of sources, they are right. If they are thinking that the study of motivations does not matter, because it does not lend itself to exact proof, they are wrong. Study of the causes of human behaviour ought to be the central purpose of the historian. Those who devote themselves to counting up Treasury tally-sticks, to making graphs of production in Cornish tin-mines, and similar scholarly pursuits, are making useful but minute additions to our factual knowledge of the past. These, in battlefield terms, are the distant tiny skirmishes. The main battle is to understand men, not their tin-mines. It would be encouraging to believe that a study of the one will lead to knowledge of the other; that a great extension of specialist studies will lead to a better understanding of the causes of human behaviour. In part this is true, though specialization easily becomes an end in itself rather than a means; but, even if that trap is avoided, there remains the intractable problem that in writing about human behaviour the historian has only partial evidence at his disposal. The most he can hope to do is to make an intelligent reconstruction of the past based on the evidence available. But, for a multitude of reasons, these reconstructions will differ from one historian to another. Historians will readily agree about the date of Magna Carta, and about its terms; these are facts. Only an incurable optimist would believe that they will ever agree over the reasons for its terms and their effects; these are matters of opinion, and opinions change as one generation of historians succeeds another.

If much of history, perhaps the most important part of it, rests on such shifting sands, how can the young historian be expected to deal with the unanswerable questions which he is set in examination-papers, unanswerable because they require judgements and opinions for which in the last resort there is no certain evidence? In practice the situation is not as dismal as it sounds. What is required of the student is not an agreed solution to the question, for the likelihood is that no such agreement exists, but intelligent use of the evidence available. It is useful for him to know the currently fashionable historical opinions and the evidence on which they are based, but if he differs from these opinions on good grounds, or sees that they are mutually contradictory, he will gain, not lose, by saying so. Dogma, however august the source, is unacceptable; it is evidence which matters.

From an early stage, therefore, the student must be prepared to make individual judgements. To do so convincingly there are certain errors, some of them of an elementary kind, which he must learn to avoid. One of these is over-statement. Absolute words—all, no one, always, never, inevitable, only—are dangerous because history is a vast subject, exceptions to generalizations are easy to find, and words such as 'never' or 'inevitable', which can be used to imply knowledge of future developments, put the writer in a false position; he is a historian not a prophet. To insist that these absolute words should be avoided altogether is pedantic and a little obtuse, but they need to be used rationally. It is worth remembering, too, that the student who weakens every statement he makes with a reservation—sometimes, in my opinion, possibly, probably, perhaps—can be equally irritating. The reader does not need to be reminded in every sentence that historical opinions are speculative; an occasional reminder at key stages is enough; common sense is the best guide.

Assessing evidence can involve more subtle difficulties than these. One springs from the ease with which preconceived ideas influence judgement. This is particularly true of the major events and characters of history. General knowledge can be particularly misleading for the young student. From the moment he starts to study the career of Napoleon he expects to find that he was a great soldier; similarly he expects to find that Joseph II was an Enlightened Despot, that Henry VIII was a self-willed opportunist, that Hitler caused the 1939-45 war. If he were a trained historian he would not *expect* to find anything. He would wait to see what the evidence was; he would pre-judge neither characters nor events. In practice this is extremely difficult, since professional historians themselves can be faulty in this way. When a small boy was asked why he could draw so well he said 'I think, then I draw round the think.' Historians sometimes write history in the same way. What tends to be missing is the uncertainty, the complexity, and the contradictory nature of personal characters and policies. Evidence has to be scrutinized carefully, and the more it seems to point universally towards the same conclusion the more sceptical the student needs to be. Was Napoleon a great soldier? What about the strategy of the Egyptian and Russian campaigns then? What about his dependence at Marengo on the good fortune of Desaix's arrival? What about his sense of timing at Waterloo? What about his neglect of new types of weapons and equipment? What about his gross misunderstanding of the difficulties of his generals in Spain? How much weight should be attached to Wellington's judgement of Napoleon? The questions could be continued but the point is plain. In history there is an abundance of evidence and counter-evidence, opinion and counter-opinion. The student has to resist the temptation to collect only that evidence which fits some pattern of explanation which he has formed in his own mind. He needs to be observant of evidence which does not fit his own pre-conceived ideas, and of evidence which does not fit the theories advanced by specialist historians. He then has to be prepared to modify his own arguments accordingly. In the end, having weighed fact A against fact B, argument X against argument Y, he may decide that one is stronger than the other, but a one-sided account which ignores the difficulties of contrary evidence is useless. It leads to stereotyped representations of characters as if they were actors in the more naïve type of Wild West film; it produces a parody of history.

If it were necessary to name one weakness which, more than any other, discredits historical judgements, it would be difficult to find one more appropriate than narrowness of vision. It is at the root of so many fallacious descriptions of the past, and it disqualifies the writer from making any sound judgement of the present. The specialist historian who believes that his particular specialist study is the most important means of arriving at the truth about the past, the nationalist historian who wishes to advertise his country's achievements, the idealistic historian who seeks evidence from the past in favour of his particular prejudices—liberalism, communism, democracy—and the student who meekly accepts one-sided accounts of the past and tabulated lists of the causes and consequences of events without probing more deeply and questioningly, all these, at their different levels, suffer from the same narrowness of vision. They do not deserve the title 'historian'.

Judgement of evidence is enlivened by occasional irony which can, in itself, exemplify the width of approach of the competent historian. Irony pinpoints the essential foolishness of an incident or attitude. At its best it shows both the detachment of the writer and his ability to judge the actions of others from the standpoint of a common sense of universal soundness. Sir Thomas More and Erasmus had this gift; so, in a different field of study, did Jane Austen. Modern historians are often endowed with the same valuable quality. Archbishop Laud's self-centred nature, for instance, is neatly portrayed in the following extract. 'When staying with his friends, his head was always "full of my business"; and the splendid banquet to which he later entertained the Court was to him a tedious business, chiefly satisfactory because none of the spoons were filched.'[1] A second example mirrors unflatteringly the narrow religious prejudices of some manufacturers in the early nineteenth century. 'There was only one God, whose name was steam and spoke in the voice of Malthus, McCulloch, and anyone who employed machinery.'[2] Original comment of this kind is not easy for the student since it is generally the product of a mature mind whose owner is confident of his knowledge and of his own standard of values; nevertheless, even if the student does no more than borrow the ironical comments of others, that at least shows an appreciation of their value.

[1] H. R. Trevor-Roper, *Archbishop Laud* (Macmillan, 1940), p. 35.
[2] E. J. Hobsbawm, *The Age of Revolution* (Weidenfeld and Nicolson, 1962), p. 186.

SECTION III

THE HISTORIAN'S ART

THE HISTORIAN'S ART

Progress by imitation is commonplace in the physical skills. The movements and methods of the outstanding figures in sport are watched with lynx-like attentiveness by the young, and imitated painstakingly, with more or less success, on playing fields all over the country. Is it possible in historical writing, with its specialized mental skills, for much of value to be learned in the same way by the study of the work of expert performers? Could a fortnight's study of A. J. P. Taylor's *History of Europe 1914-1945* perform the same service for the young historian as a fortnight at Wimbledon performs for the young tennis player? Obviously in both something depends on the experience and natural abilities of the watcher; equally it is clear that from the cradle onwards imitation of good models is an important part of the process of learning. There should be advantages, therefore, in studying the works of outstanding historians, not only for their subject-matter, but also for their style, their techniques, and their qualities of judgement. Probably few would dispute this.

Acceptance of the value of imitation is, in part, the justification for the publication of books of extracts from leading historians. Up to a point these are useful, though if they are to be any more than coffee-table or bedside reading they need to be accompanied by a critical commentary. The methods by which given effects are achieved need to be explicitly shown. Furthermore, the habit of giving a series of extracts without comment from the writings of Thucydides, Clarendon, Gibbon, Macaulay, and so on, through to the present day, can be actively misleading for the young student in that fashions in style and method change. Gibbon's monumental generalizations, Macaulay's partiality for moral judgements, and Motley's elaborately constructed metaphors, have a curiosity value and are worth the young historian's attention as part of his education in the subject, but he would be unwise if he attempted to imitate the methods of these writers exactly. Nevertheless the writings of the leading historians of the past have sufficient qualities of permanence to make them of interest still. Along with much which a modern historian would jettison, for historical or literary reasons, there remains in them a nucleus of thought which is as freshly significant for the student now as it was when it was first written. This quality can only be briefly glimpsed in extracts, but the following excerpts show something of the characteristic styles of Gibbon, Macaulay, and Motley, who have been taken as examples of a style of historical writing which is recognizably distinct from the styles now favoured. At the end of each extract there are questions. Some of them are matters of interpretation, but the answers suggested to these and the later extracts will be found on p. 138.

Extract 1

The rise of a city, which swelled into an empire, may deserve, as a singular prodigy, the reflection of a philosophical mind. But the decline of Rome was the natural and inevitable effect of immoderate greatness. Prosperity ripened the principle of decay; the causes of destruction multiplied with the extent of conquest; and as soon as time or accident had removed the artificial supports, the stupendous fabric yielded to the pressure of its own weight. The story of its ruin is simple and obvious; and instead of inquiring *why* the Roman empire was destroyed, we should rather be surprised that it had subsisted so long. The victorious legions, who, in distant wars, acquired the vices of strangers and mercenaries, first oppressed the freedom of the republic, and afterwards violated the majesty of the purple. The emperors, anxious for their personal safety and the public peace, were reduced to the base expedient of corrupting the discipline which rendered them alike formidable to their sovereign and to the enemy; the vigour of the military government was relaxed and finally dissolved by the partial institutions of Constantine; and the Roman world was overwhelmed by a deluge of barbarians.

The decay of Rome has been frequently ascribed to the translation of the seat of empire; but this history has already shown that the powers of government were *divided* rather than *removed*. The throne of Constantinople was erected in the East; while the West was still possessed by a series of emperors who held their residence in Italy, and claimed their equal inheritance of the legions and provinces. This dangerous novelty impaired the strength and fomented the vices of a double reign: the instruments of an oppressive and arbitrary system were multiplied; and a vain emulation of luxury, not of merit, was introduced and supported between the degenerate successors of Theodosius. Extreme distress, which unites the virtue of a free people, embitters the factions of a declining monarchy. The hostile favourites of Arcadius and Honorius betrayed the republic to its common enemies; and the Byzantine court beheld with indifference, perhaps with pleasure, the disgrace of Rome, the misfortune of Italy, and the loss of the West. Under the succeeding reigns the alliance of the two empires was restored; but the aid of the Oriental Romans was tardy, doubtful, and ineffectual; and the national schism of the Greeks and Latins was enlarged by the perpetual difference of language and manners, of interests, and even of religion. Yet the salutary event approved in some measure of judgement of Constantine. During a long period of decay his impregnable city repelled the victorious armies of barbarians, protected the wealth of Asia, and commanded, both in peace and war, the important straits which connect the Euxine and Mediterranean seas. The foundation of Constantinople more essentially contributed to the preservation of the East than to the ruin of the West.

E. Gibbon, *The Decline and Fall of the Roman Empire* (Abridged edition, ed. H. Trevor-Roper, New English Library, 1966), pp. 274-6.

Questions

1. Are there any words or phrases which would be out of place in modern writing?

2. What evidence within the passage suggests that Gibbon may generalize too readily?

3. What are the merits of the style?

4. The power to analyse ideas critically is one of the marks of sound historical writing. Is there any evidence of this quality in the extract?

Extract 2

In the meantime the Prussian forces had been assembled. Without any declaration of war, without any demand for reparation, in the very act of pouring forth compliments and assurances of good will, Frederick commenced hostilities. Many thousands of his troops were actually in Silesia before the Queen of Hungary knew that he had set up any claim to any part of her territories. At length he sent her a message which could be regarded only as an insult. If she would but let him have Silesia, he would, he said, stand by her against any power which should try to deprive her of her other dominions; as if he was not already bound to stand by her, or as if his new promise could be of more value than the old one.

It was the depth of winter. The cold was severe, and the roads heavy with mire. But the Prussians pressed on. Resistance was impossible. The Austrian army was then neither numerous nor efficient. The small portion of that army which lay in Silesia was unprepared for hostilities. Glogau was blockaded; Breslau opened its gates; Ohlau was evacuated. A few scattered garrisons still held out; but the whole open country was subjugated: no enemy ventured to encounter the King in the field; and, before the end of January 1741, he returned to receive the congratulations of his subjects at Berlin.

Had the Silesian question been merely a question between Frederick and Maria Theresa, it would be impossible to acquit the Prussian King of gross perfidy. But when we consider the effects which his policy produced, and could not fail to produce, on the whole community of civilized nations, we are compelled to pronounce a condemnation still more severe. Till he began the war, it seemed possible, even probable, that the peace of the world would be preserved. The plunder of the great Austrian heritage was indeed a strong temptation; and in more than one cabinet ambitious schemes were already meditated. But the treaties by which the Pragmatic Sanction had been guaranteed were express and recent. To throw all Europe into confusion for a purpose clearly unjust, was no light matter. England was true to her engagements. The voice of Fleury had always been for peace. He had a conscience. He was now in extreme old age, and was unwilling, after a life which, when his situation was considered, must be pronounced singularly pure, to carry the fresh stain of a great crime before the tribunal of his God. Even the vain and unprincipled Belle-Isle, whose whole life was one wild day-dream of conquest and spoilation, felt that France, bound as she was by solemn stipulations, could not, without disgrace, make a direct attack on the Austrian dominions. Charles, Elector of Bavaria, pretended that he had a right to a large part of the inheritance which the Pragmatic Sanction gave to the Queen of Hungary; but he was not sufficiently powerful to move without support. It might, therefore, not unreasonably be expected that, after a short period of restlessness, all the potentates of Christendom would acquiesce in the arrangements made by the late Emperor. But the selfish rapacity of the King of Prussia gave the signal to his neighbours. His example quieted their sense of shame. His success led them to underrate the difficulty of dismembering the Austrian monarchy. The whole world sprang to arms. On the head of Frederick is all the blood which was shed in a war which raged during many years and in every quarter of the globe, the blood of the column of Fontenoy, the blood of the mountaineers who were slaughtered at Culloden. The evils produced by his wickedness were felt in lands where the name of Prussia was unknown; and in order that he might rob a neighbour whom he had promised to defend, black men fought on the coast of Coromandel, and red men scalped each other by the Great Lakes of North America.

> Lord Macaulay, *Critical and Historical Essays* (London: Longmans, 1883), p. 667.

Questions

1. In what ways does the sentence structure of this passage help Macaulay to achieve the effects he wants?

2. Macaulay had fewer misgivings than modern historians in passing strong moral judgements. Which sentences illustrate this point? Why is there a greater reluctance now to pass judgements of this kind?

Extract 3

That convention was signed in the spring of 1609. The ten ensuing years in Europe were comparatively tranquil, but they were scarcely to be numbered among the full and fruitful sheaves of a pacific epoch. It was a pause, a breathing spell during which the sulphurous clouds which had made the atmosphere of Christendom poisonous for nearly half a century had sullenly rolled away, while at every point of the horizon they were seen massing themselves anew in portentous and ever accumulating strength. At any moment the faint and sickly sunshine in which poor exhausted Humanity was essaying a feeble twitter of hope as it plumed itself for a peaceful flight might be again obscured. To us of a remote posterity the momentary division of epochs seems hardly discernible. So rapidly did that fight of Demons which we call the Thirty Years' War tread on the heels of the forty years' struggle for Dutch Independence which had just been suspended that we are accustomed to think and speak of the Eighty [*sic*] Years' War as one pure perfect sanguinary whole.

And indeed the Tragedy which was soon to sweep solemnly across Europe was foreshadowed in the first fitful years of peace. The throb of the elementary forces already shook the soil of Christendom. The fantastic but most significant conflict in the territories of the dead Duke of Cleve reflected the distant and gigantic war as in a mirage. It will be necessary to direct the reader's attention at the proper moment to that episode, for it was one in which the beneficent sagacity of Barneveld was conspicuously exerted in the cause of peace and conservation. Meantime it is not agreeable to reflect that this brief period of nominal and armed peace which the Republic had conquered after nearly two generations of warfare was employed by her in tearing her own flesh. The heroic sword which had achieved such triumphs in the cause of freedom could have been better employed than in an attempt at political suicide.

> J. L. Motley, *Life and Death of John of Barneveld*, Vol. 1 (Murray, 1904), pp. 4f.

Question

1. Metaphors can add valuably to the impact made in writing. Do they do so here? Explain your opinion.

Extract 4

Had John of Barneveld's counsels been always followed, had illustrious birth placed him virtually upon a throne, as was the case with William the Silent, and thus allowed him occasionally to carry out the designs of a great mind with almost despotic authority, it might have been better for the world. But in that age, it was royal blood alone that could command unflinching obedience without exciting personal rivalry. Men quailed before his majestic intellect, but hated him for the power which was its necessary result. They already felt a stupid delight in cavilling at his pedigree. To dispute his claim to a place among the ancient nobility to which he was an honour was to revenge themselves for the rank he unquestionably possessed side by side in all but birth with the kings and rulers of the world. Whether envy and jealousy be vices more incident to the republican form of government than to other political systems may be an open question. But it is no question whatever that Barneveld's every footstep from this period forward was dogged by envy as patient as it was devouring. Jealousy stuck to him like his shadow. We have examined the relations which existed between Winwood and himself; we have seen that ambassador, now secretary of state for James, never weary in denouncing the Advocate's haughtiness and grim resolution to govern the country according to its laws rather than at the dictate of a foreign sovereign, and in flinging forth malicious insinuations in regard to his relations to Spain. The man whose every hour was devoted—in spite of a thousand obstacles strewn by stupidity, treachery, and apathy, as well as by envy, hatred, and bigotry—to the organizing of a grand and universal league of Protestantism against Spain, and to rolling up with strenuous and sometimes despairing arms a dead mountain weight, ever ready to fall back upon and crush him, was accused in dark and mysterious whispers, soon to grow louder and bolder, of a treacherous inclination for Spain.

There is nothing less surprising nor more sickening for those who observe public life, and wish to retain faith in the human species, than the almost infinite power of the meanest of passions.

J. L. Motley, op. cit., pp. 382f.

Questions

1. Is the use of metaphor and simile more effective in this extract than in the previous one? Why?

2. Moral generalizations occur frequently in the work of nineteenth century historians. What examples can you find here? Are these generalizations 'fair comment'?

3. What are the merits of Motley's style?

Much of writing and thinking is essentially imitative; even writers more self-conscious about style than historians tend to be are seldom completely original. Historical style is influenced, as other writing is, by the outlook and literary habits of the writer's own period. It is influenced too by the writer's personal background and environment, and often by his conscious modelling of his own writing upon an admired style. In the extracts which follow each author's writing has traces of the style to be found in the works of Gibbon and Macaulay. There is a concern, overmuch concern, with the careful shaping of phrases to secure literary effect. The author's own opinions are obtrusively present, and are not always backed with convincing, or any, evidence. There is a tendency to oversimplify, so that historical situations and characters are treated as if they were excerpts from a Victorian melodrama, its heroes unbelievably heroic, its villains unbelievably villainous. Both historians, Froude and Trevelyan, were men of insight and imagination, qualities which can be as important as diligent factual research in assessing the past, but in the passages selected there seems to be an artificiality of sound and sense which weakens the power of their writing.

Extract 5

It is well to pause and look for a moment at this small band of heroes (i.e. the London Protestants who distributed Tyndale's translation of the Scriptures); for heroes they were, if ever men deserved the name. Unlike the first reformers who had followed Wycliffe, they had no earthly object, emphatically none; and equally unlike them, perhaps, because they had no earthly object, they were all, as I have said, poor men—either students, like Tyndale, or artisans and labourers who worked for their own bread, and in tough contact with reality, had learnt better than the great and the uneducated the difference between truth and lies. Wycliffe had royal dukes and noblemen for his supporters—knights and divines among his disciples—a King and a House of Commons looking upon him, not without favour. The first Protestants of the sixteenth century had for their king the champion of Holy Church, who had broken a lance with Luther; and spiritual rulers over them alike powerful and imbecile, whose highest conception of Christian virtue was the destruction of those who disobeyed their mandates. The masses of the people were indifferent to a cause which promised them no material advantage; and the Commons of Parliament, while contending with the abuses of the spiritual authorities, were laboriously anxious to wash their hands of heterodoxy. 'In the crime of heresy, thanked be God,' said the bishops in 1529, 'there hath no notable person fallen in our time;' no chief priest, chief ruler, or learned Pharisee—not one. 'Truth it is that certain apostate friars and monks, lewd priests, bankrupt merchants, vagabonds and lewd idle fellows of corrupt nature, have embraced the abominable and erroneous opinions lately sprung in Germany, and by them have been some seduced. Against these, if judgement have been exercised according to the laws of the realm, we be without blame. If we have been too remiss, or slack, we shall gladly do our duty henceforth.' Such were the first Protestants in the eyes of their superiors. On one side was wealth, rank, dignity, the weight of authority, the majority of numbers, the prestige of centuries; here too were the phantom legions of superstition and cowardice; and here were all the worthier influences so pre-eminently English, which lead wise men to shrink from change, and to cling to things established, so long as one stone of them remains upon another. This was the army of conservatism. Opposed to it were a little band of enthusiasts, armed only with truth and fearlessness; 'weak things of the world,' about to do battle in God's name; and it was to be seen whether God or the world was the stronger. They were armed, I say, with the truth. It was that alone which could have given them victory in so uneven a struggle. They had returned to the essential fountain of life; they re-asserted the principle which has lain at the root of all religions, whatever their name or outward form, which once burnt with divine lustre in that

Catholicism which was now to pass away; the fundamental axiom of all real life, that the service which man owes to God is not the service of words or magic forms, or ceremonies or opinions; but the service of holiness, of purity, of obedience to the everlasting laws of duty.

> J. A. Froude, *History of England* (Longmans, 1893) Vol. 1, pp. 510-12.

Questions

1 What instances can you find of overstatement?

2. In making a contrast of the kind shown in the last part of the passage i.e. enthusiasts against conservatives there is a danger. What is it?

3. Are the writer's opinions too obtrusive and if so what personal sympathies (or prejudices) do they reveal?

4. What are the merits of the style?

Extract 6

Garibaldi had, perhaps, the most romantic life that history records, for it had all the trappings as well as the essence of romance. Though he lived in the nineteenth century, it was yet his fortune never to take part in the full prose life of civilized men, and so he never understood it, though he moved it profoundly, like a great wind blowing off an unknown shore. He never had education, either intellectual, diplomatic, or political; even his military training was that of a guerrilla chief; nor, till he was past learning, did he experience the ordinary life of the settled citizen. Though all must acknowledge that, by the secret ordering of the mysteries of birth, he had been created with more in him of the divine than any training can give, yet we cannot fail to perceive, in studying the slight records of the first forty years of his life, how much the natural tendencies of his genius, in their strength and in their weakness, were enhanced by circumstance.

And so, when in 1848 he returned to fight for Italy, in the full strength of matured manhood—at the time of life when Cromwell first drew sword—he had been sheltered, ever since he went to sea at fifteen, from every influence which might have turned him into an ordinary man or an ordinary soldier.

He had had two schools—the seas of romance and the plateaus of South America. He had lived on ship-board and in the saddle. The man who loved Italy as even she has seldom been loved, scarcely knew her. The soldier of modern enlightenment was himself but dimly enlightened. Rather, his mind was like a vast sea-cave, filled with the murmur of dark waters at flow and the stirring of nature's forces, lit here and there by streaks of glorious sunshine bursting in through crevices hewn at random in its rugged sides. He had all the distinctive qualities of the hero, in their highest possible degree, and in their very simplest form. Courage and endurance without limit; tenderness to man and to all living things, which was never blunted by a lifetime of war in two hemispheres among combatants often but half civilized; the power to fill men with ardour by his presence and to stir them by his voice to great deeds; but above all the passion to be striking a blow for the oppressed, a passion which could not be quenched by failure, nor checked by reason, nor sated by success, old age, and the worship of the world.

These qualities, perhaps, could not have existed in a degree so pre-eminent, in the person either of a sage or of a saint. Without, on the one hand, the child-like simplicity that often degenerated into folly, and on the other hand, the full store of common human passions that made him one with the multitude, he could never have been so ignorant of despair and doubt, so potent to overawe his enemies, to spread his own infectious daring among his followers and to carry men blindfold into enterprises which would have been madness under any other chief. The crowning work of his life was in 1860, when he landed with a thousand ill-armed volunteers in the island of Sicily, to overcome a garrison of 24,000 well-armed and well-disciplined men. Moltke could no more have conquered Sicily with such means, than Garibaldi could have planned the battle of Sedan.

G. M. Trevelyan, *Garibaldi* (London: Longmans, 1933), pp. 23-5.

Questions

1. This passage could be criticized in that, at some points, Trevelyan is striving too obviously after literary effect. At which points could this criticism be made, and with what justice?

2. The writer occasionally uses long sentences. Does he control the movement of ideas within them effectively and, if so, how?

3. The writer has a gift for historical comparisons. Where does this show itself, and what is the value of making comparisons in this way?

4. 'He had lived on ship-board and in the saddle.' What is the merit of this method of expression?

5. Biographers are apt to become too sympathetic to their subjects.

Is there any evidence to suggest that this may be happening in this excerpt?

Of the extracts given so far the most recent is from a book published in 1933. At some points the style and approach of these writers have seemed vulnerable to criticism. This was not intended as a prelude to universal praise of modern historians, nor to universal criticism of earlier historians. Historical techniques and styles of expression have changed, and probably for the better, though allowance has to be made for the fact that in specialized studies there is a tendency to be over-critical about the work of one's predecessors and too complacent about one's own. Certainly it would be a mistake for the student to think that all historical writing in the early nineteenth and twentieth centuries was full of pretentious phrases and glib moral judgements. The next three extracts, taken from the period 1888 to 1908, should help to correct that impression. Here and there individual words and phrases reflect the period in which they were written, but all the extracts carry conviction as pieces of historical writing because they have an immediately recognizable soundness of judgement which is common ground amongst all historians of outstanding calibre at whatever period they are writing.

Extract 7

We may trace in such records (of Anselm's life at the monastery of Bec) that remarkable combination of qualities which ultimately made Anselm the object of a love and reverence surpassing even the admiration excited by his rare genius. What is striking is that with so much of his age, so powerful and severe a mind, so stern in his individual life, a monk of the monks, a dogmatist of the dogmatists, he yet had so much beyond his age; he was not only so gentle and affectionate and self-forgetting, but he was so considerate, so indulgent, so humane, so free-spirited, so natural. Austerity was part of the ordinary religious type of the time; it went, indeed, commonly with all loftiness of character and aim; the great Conqueror was austere, and of course a monk with a high estimate of his calling was so. But Anselm's almost light-hearted cheerfulness, his winning and informal nature, his temper of moderation and good sense, his interest in all kinds of men, and power of accommodating himself to all kinds of characters, his instinctive insight into the substance of questions of truth and justice, his leaning in an age when all trust was placed in unbending rules, to the side of compassion and liberty, formed a combination with personal austerity with which his age was not familiar. His place of work was among monks, and he must not be regarded as a popular teacher of religion. He had gifts which, perhaps, might have qualified him to exercise a wide popular influence; but he lived in times when there was little thought of direct addresses to the minds of the multitude, and when all serious efforts at ordering life on religious principles were concentrated in a small body of professed ascetics. The days of the great preachers were at hand; but they had not yet come. A certain number of homilies are found among Anselm's works; but they are for the most part of doubtful authority, and those which seem genuine are not sermons, but expositions, meant not for a lay congregation, but for a chapter-house of monks. Yet it is clear that Anselm's influence told on numbers who were not monks; and the vehicle of his influence seems to have been, not preaching, but free conversation. To his passion for abstract and profound thought, he joined a taste for simple and natural explanation, and a homely humour in illustration, which reminds the reader sometimes of Luther or Latimer—more truly, perhaps, of St. François de Sales, and of the vein of quaint and unceremonious amusement running through some of the later Italian works of devotion. Eadmer, or some other of his friends, made a collection of his sayings and comparisons, and his common modes of presenting moral and religious topics, very miscellaneous in selection and unequal in worth, but giving probably an unstudied representation of his ordinary manner of discourse. 'He taught,' says Eadmer, 'not as is the wont with others, but in a widely different fashion, setting forth each point under common and familiar examples, and supporting it by the strength of solid reasons, without any veils or disguises of speech.'

R. W. Church, *Saint Anselm* (Macmillan, 1888), pp. 96-8.

Questions

1. This is writing of considerable strength and impetus. Balanced phrasing, massing of phrases, choice of words, and subtle punctuation help to achieve this. Give examples.

2. The 'asides' of historians often reveal the depth of their knowledge and thought about the periods of which they have special knowledge. How is this shown in this extract?

3. Character assessments are of little value unless they are firmly rooted in documentary evidence. Does the extract suggest that Church attaches great importance to this type of evidence?

Extract 8

It is one of the penalties which great men must pay for their greatness, that they have to be judged by posterity according to a standard which they themselves could not have recognized, because it was by their greatness that the standard itself was created. Henry V may be judged and condemned on moral principles which have emerged from the age in which he was a great actor, but which that age neither knew nor practised. He renewed a great war, which according to modern ideas was without justification in its origin and continuance, and which resulted in an exhaustion from which the nation did not recover for a century. To modern minds war seems a terrible evil, to be incurred only on dire necessity where honour or existence is at stake; to be justified only by the clearest demonstration of right; to be continued not a moment longer than the moral necessity continues. Perhaps no war ancient or modern has been so waged, justified, or concluded; men both spoke and thought otherwise in earlier times, and in times not so very far distant from our own. For medieval warfare it might be pleaded, that its legal justifications were as a rule far more complete than were the excuses with which Louis XIV and Frederick II defended their aggressive designs; for the kings of the middle ages went to war for rights, not for interests, much less for ideas. But it must be further remembered, that until comparatively late times, although the shedding of Christian blood was constantly deplored, war was regarded as the highest and noblest work of kings; and that in England, the history of which must have been Henry's guide, the only three unwarlike kings who had reigned since the Conquest had been despised and set aside by their subjects. The war with France was not to him a new war; it had lasted far beyond the memory of any living man, and the nation had been educated into the belief that the struggle was one condition of its normal existence. The royal house, we may be sure, had been thoroughly instructed in all the minutiae of their claims; the parliament insists as strongly on the royal rights as on its own privileges; and the fall of Henry VI shows how fatal to any dynasty must have been the renunciation of those rights. The blame of continuing the war when success was hopeless, if such blame be just, does not fall on Henry V, who died at the culminating point of his successes, and whose life, if it had been prolonged, might have consolidated what he had won. Judged by the standard of his time, judged by the standard according to which later ages have acted, even whilst they recognized its imperfection, Henry V cannot be condemned for the iniquity or for the final and fatal results of his military policy. He believed war to be right, he believed in his own cause, he devoted himself to his work and he accomplished it.

W. Stubbs, *The Constitutional History of England*
(Oxford: the Clarendon Press, 1890), Vol. III, pp. 75f.

1. Bishop Stubbs is here describing an important element in historical judgement. What is it? Is the argument advanced convincingly?

2. Does the last sentence make a strong finish? Comment.

Extract 9

And first we will observe that in this country any talk of a feudal
system is a comparatively new thing: I should say that we do not
hear of a feudal system until long after feudalism had ceased to exist.
From the end of the seventeenth century onwards our English law
grew up in wonderful isolation: it became very purely English and
insular. Our lawyers seem to have known little and cared nothing
about the law of foreign countries, nothing about Roman jurisprudence.
Their English authorities were all sufficient for them, and neither our
parliaments nor our courts were subjected to any foreign influence.
Coke in his voluminous works has summed up for us the law of the
later Middle Ages, but in all his books, unless I am mistaken, there
is no word about the feudal system. If, we may say, he expounds that
system in full detail so far as that system was English, he is quite
unconscious that he is doing anything of the kind; he has no thought
of a system common to the nations of Europe, he is speaking of our
insular law. No, for 'a feudal system' we must turn from Coke to a
contemporary of his, that learned and laborious antiquary, Sir Henry
Spelman. Coke was born in 1552 and died in 1633; Spelman was born
in 1562 and died in 1641: so they were just contemporaries. Now
were an examiner to ask who introduced the feudal system into England? one very good answer, if properly explained, would be Henry
Spelman, and if there followed the question, what was the feudal
system? a good answer to that would be, an early essay in comparative jurisprudence. Spelman reading continental books saw that
English law, for all its insularity, was a member of a great European
family, a family between all the members of which there are strong
family likenesses. This was for Englishmen a grand and striking dis-
covery; much that had seemed quite arbitrary in their old laws, now
seemed explicable. They learned of feudal law as of a medieval *ius
gentium*, a system common to all the nations of the West. The new
learning was propagated among English lawyers by Sir Martin Wright;
it was popularized and made orthodox by Blackstone in his easy
attractive manner. If my examiner went on with his questions and
asked me, when did the feudal system attain its most perfect development? I should answer about the middle of the last century. It was
then, I should add that the notion of one grand idea and a few simple
principles underlying the mass of medieval law, English and con-

tinental, was firmly grasped and used as a means of exploring all that seemed to need explanation in the old English law. Now this was an important step—this connecting of English with foreign law, this endeavour to find some general intelligible principles running through the terrible tangle of our old books. Most undoubtedly there was much in our old law which could be explained only by reference to ideas which had found a completer development beyond seas, and to Blackstone and to Wright, and above all to Spelman, we owe a heavy debt. But since Blackstone's day we have learned and unlearned many things about the Middle Ages. In particular we have learned to see vast differences as well as striking resemblances, to distinguish countries and to distinguish times. If now we speak of the feudal system, it should be with a full understanding that the feudalism of France differs radically from the feudalism of England, that the feudalism of the thirteenth is very different from that of the eleventh century. The phrase has thus become for us so large and vague that it is quite possible to maintain that of all countries England was the most, or for the matter of that the least, feudalized; that William the Conqueror introduced, or for the matter of that suppressed, the feudal system.

> F. W. Maitland, *The Constitutional History of England* (Cambridge University Press, 1908), pp. 141-3.

Questions

1. The power and originality of Maitland's scholarship are renowned. What evidence is there of these qualities in this extract?

2. Maitland's style is not necessarily beyond criticism. Is there any weakness evident?

Although the work of the historians so far quoted in this chapter can be instructive for the student, most of his reading will be of the work of modern historians. Since style is largely imitative, students are more likely to base their literary methods, consciously or unconsciously, on those of present day historians rather than on those of the past. For the most part their work will not be any the worse for that. There are some qualities of permanence in style, as Shakespeare and the translators of the Bible have shown, but even with these classic exceptions the flavour of much that they wrote was probably best appreciated by the audiences and readers of their own times. Certainly there are passages in Gibbon and Macaulay, and even in Motley and Trevelyan, which now seem dated and inappropriate in historical writing. The major advantage of past historians over more recent ones is that the work of only the best of them has survived whereas modern historians are prolifically present in print. The student therefore needs to develop some sense of discrimination. Good historical writing has clarity and interest; bad historical writing has not.

If that were the end of the matter the task of the student would be simple. In practice, however, there are strongly opposed views about the qualities required to write history effectively. One view is that an attractive style is of little importance, and may even be positively harmful in that it may tempt the author to pay more attention to vivid expression of ideas than to historical fact. This puritanical approach was, and is, valuable as a corrective to the romantic approach of the literary historians, but it is itself vulnerable to criticism. Unless the historian communicates his knowledge he is merely an irrelevance in society, yet as soon as he does communicate his knowledge his style becomes of significance. It is perfectly possible to write effectively without adorning the work with purple passages and poetic extracts; the natural rhythm of a well-developed argument can be of compulsive interest; but when the historian achieves this he is showing his capacity as a literary stylist as well as a historian. Simplicity may be the highest form of style though, artistically, it needs the relief of contrast to be wholly effective. What the student does need to avoid, however, is imitation of those modern historians who are capable of neither literary ingenuity, which they despise, nor of lucidity, which perhaps they despise too. Fortunately there are many historians who combine historical and literary ability to an exceptional degree as the following extracts, mainly from modern works, show. Others could have been chosen to illustrate the point but the selection was partly made with the object of finding a variety of subject-matter.

Extract 10

London was a huge port and a huge town and, at its worst, as dark and wicked as such towns are. In the porch of St. Paul's in the arcaded shopping centre of the New Exchange, the 'coney catcher' loitered to ensnare some wide-eyed country rabbit with a little money in his foolish paws. The 'jeering, cunning courtesan, the rooking, roaring boy' conspired to wheedle and bully unsuspecting fools. All day the shouts

of oyster and tripe women, the swearing of draymen, the creak and
clatter of hackney coaches dazed and deafened the newcomer, and
after sunset

> 'riotous sinful plush and tell-tale spurs
> Walk Fleet Street and the Strand, when the soft stirs
> Of bawdry ruffled silks turn night to day.'

London was not a safe place for the innocent, although those accustomed to it, born in 'the scent of Newcastle coal and the hearing of
Bow bells', knew how to avoid the dangers, and the more experienced
revellers who came in for a spree, like Sir Humphrey Mildmay who
got home 'mad, merry and late' after 'playing the fool with two
punks in a barge on the Thames,' were very well able to take care of
themselves. But country boys and girls, driven to the capital by bad
times or tempted by tales of easy money, drifted through disappoint-
ment and disaster into the criminal depths of the city, to die in the
common gaol or of the 'Tyburn ague' on the gallows.

As the town grew, and it was growing fast, its gaieties increased.
Bear gardens and pleasure gardens spread along Bankside, puppet-
theatres showed *Bel and the Dragon* and other apocryphal matter;
peep-shows advertised *The Creation of the World* represented to the
life in pasteboard. The two principal theatres, now both covered in
and lit by wax candles, attracted the rich and fashionable. Blackfriars on
Bankside carried on the Shakespeare—Burbage tradition, with Taylor,
thought to be the greatest Hamlet yet seen, and Swanston's much
praised Othello; the portly comedian Lowin played Falstaff and the
whole Jonsonian gallery of grotesques, and the fair youth Stephen
Hammerton drew tears with his Juliet and Desdemona. Christopher
Beeston's company at the Cockpit in Drury Lane concentrated on
more modern typical works. These two had the highest reputation
though half a dozen lesser theatres, more old-fashioned, open-roofed
and playing by daylight, still drew large audiences. A French company
brought over the neo-classical drama from Paris but the Londoners,
taking it into their heads to be scandalized at seeing women on the
stage, pelted them with rotten apples. The Queen, who patronized the
company was indignant, and after a little the Londoners forgot their
moral views and accepted the novelty.

The tidal Thames, creeping into the heart of the city up many an
open inlet, ditch and hithe, did something to purify the town. Fresh
water had been brought within reach by the New River Company
which had diverted the River Lea to Islington. But rosemary and
jasmine were in constant demand to disguise the putrid smells of
streets and houses. London children already suffered badly from
rickets, and the various epidemic diseases vaguely defined as plague
caused ten thousand deaths in the bad year 1636. In the following year,

still bad, there were something over three thousand victims.

The respectable citizens of London drew together against the under-world of the criminal, the drunken, the defeated. Their city might be one of the wickedest in Europe; it was also, as a natural consequence, one of the most austerely pious. The virtues of plain living and hard work were extolled and practised; the Bible and the hundred churches stood firm against the ballads and the playhouses. Religion was a fighting force in the city because it could never cease from fighting, 'the miles between Hell and any other place on earth being shorter than those between London and St. Albans.'

> C. V. Wedgwood, *The King's Peace, 1637-41* (Collins 1955), pp. 31-3.

Questions

1. Comment on the use of quotations.

2. This extract contains very effective descriptive writing. What is its main source of strength?

Extract 11

For three-quarters of a century before 1714, England had been a byword for political instability. She had passed through the crucible of civil war, executed her King, abolished and then returned to monar-chical government, expelled the restored dynasty and repudiated the hereditary right to the crown, and placed first a Dutch and then a German sovereign on the throne held by a purely parliamentary title. Her constitution had successively taken the forms of personal monarchy, of republicanism under parliamentary and later under military direc- tion, and finally of an ill-defined dualism between a Crown theoretically supreme in matters of administration and policy and a Parliament sovereign in matters of legislation and finance. Internally, the country had been convulsed by rebellion, conspiracy, and a war of parties the 'mercilessness' of which gave evidence of their inability to agree on the fundamental principles underlying the organization of either State or Church. Though England had survived the ordeal of recurrent warfare abroad, to emerge the dominant European power of the early eighteenth century, her security within the island system itself had been impaired by conflicts, both military and political, with her Scottish neighbour. The recovery of Ireland had, in 1649 and again in 1689, twice to be undertaken. England's weakness and instability had, at these moments of crisis, impaired her control over her colonial possessions. Yet, im-probable as such an outcome might have seemed, the accession in

1714 of an elderly and unprepossessing German prince, ignorant alike of the language and character of his new kingdom and profoundly attached to his Hanoverian electorate, ushered in an age of almost unbroken internal tranquillity and external progress.

> D. L. Keir, *The Constitutional History of Modern Britain 1485-1951* (A. and C. Black, 1964), pp. 289-90.

Question

This passage makes an effective introduction to the reign of George I. Why?

Extract 12

. . . Old Sir Robert had projected his still unconsumed will and ambition into his first and brilliant son's career, sparing neither money nor influence on his behalf. He had his reward when he read Robert's speeches in the press or invited his Staffordshire neighbours to dine with the Home Secretary at Drayton. But for the son this silent and subconscious pressure had its reverse-side. The perpetual knowledge of the expectations formed of him could scarcely have failed to lay a burden on Peel which was made even more onerous by his own pride and ambition. For an imaginative man these were heavy burdens to carry. Masterful as Peel was in action, he was often curiously nervous beforehand. It showed in small ways: in his fit of depression before his degree examination, and in the characteristic expressions of apprehension when accepting the Irish Secretaryship in 1812 and in the Home Office in 1821. Hardinge noted that Peel as leader of the House of Commons 'had a sad want of moral courage before the debate, but once in for it his physical courage carried him on'. This contrast between the mental anticipation and the actual event was a reflection of the contradictory forces within.

In Peel's nature there was in fact a discordancy between the inner person and the person he presented to the world. He had created, perhaps had always had to create, an artificial self with which to deal with others. It was this dualism which explains the widely different views about him held by his friends and his critics. But though Peel had perhaps created this secondary personality as a form of protection for himself, use and habit had made it a second nature; and it is not surprising that observers often failed to distinguish between the two. Moreover, vulnerability has its own methods of retaliation. The need for self-protection easily enlists less amiable qualities on its side; and of these Peel had his full share. His humour tended to be secretive and sometimes malicious; his detachment from others bred contempt;

his integrity could degenerate into self-righteousness; the unnecessary emphasis on the purity of his motives made him on occasion sancti-monious. Ingrowing virtues have a trick of developing ingrowing vices; and though Peel saw much of the world, he held himself too con-sciously apart from it. The very success and ease of his career distilled their own subtle poisons. He never had to struggle; and he had too much scorn for politicians who could less afford to be nice in the methods they used in making their careers. He was above temptation; and had too little sympathy for the human motives behind the petty political dishonesty he constantly witnessed. He never had to court patronage of powerful ministers; and he let himself too readily despise the flattery and supplication which were the weapons of lesser men. These, in the political world of the early nineteenth century, were no doubt faults on the right side and it could be argued that what the world needed was more Robert Peels and fewer ordinary politicians. But politics, like the world itself, is made up of ordinary men. Only a person of great humility could have held Peel's standards and retained complete humanity; and Peel was not humble. He lacked therefore the natural touch which is one of the most endearing traits of human beings. There was nothing in Peel comparable to the earthiness of Walpole, the simplicity of Fox, the cynicism of Melbourne, or the insouciance of Palmerston. To speak of him as though he were above all a great House of Commons man is misleading; he commanded their respect but rarely their devotion.

N. Gash, *Mr. Secretary Peel* (Longmans, 1961), pp. 666-8.

Questions

1. The most striking feature of this writing is the sense of balance created both in judgement and style. How is this achieved?

2. The writer is apt to use 'and' after a semi-colon. Does this weaken the impact of his writing?

Extract 13

Such doubts (by Hitler of Himmler's efficiency) were not left un-exploited by the patient, persistent Bormann. This 'evil genius of the Fuehrer', this 'Brown Eminence, sitting in the shadows', as one of the court described him, 'Hitler's Mephistopheles', as he was more generally known, had by now achieved an undisputed supremacy such as had never previously been known in the immediate *entourage* of his master. Hitherto it had been, or at least it had seemed, Hitler's policy never to allow any of his ministers to attain to any singularity of position in his counsels. He had seemed always to play off one minister against another, and so himself to hold the balance among them. But now Martin Bormann, who, like Holstein in the cabinets of the Kaiser, had 'realized from the beginning the importance of representing his position as insignificant', had won the reward of his infinite patience. Never away from his master's side, even keeping the same eccentric hours as he,—rising at midday and retiring at 4.30 or 5 in the morning, —in sole control of the vast machinery of the Party, indispensable, indefatigable, and ubiquitous, he was now the sole custodian of Hitler's secrets, the sole channel for his orders, the sole method of approach to that ever more inaccessible presence. During the years of war every development had strengthened his authority. The Gauleiters had been old Party hacks who, having thumped their tubs and blown their trumpets obstreperously in the early days of the movement, had been rewarded with these lucrative and not too exacting offices. Bormann had changed that. One by one the old Gauleiters had gone, and new men had replaced them, younger, more energetic more fanatical men, who owed everything not to the impersonal Party in the days when Bormann was unknown, but to Bormann himself. Throughout the war the Party machine, like the S.S. had grown; like the S.S. it had encroached on the functions of the Armed Forces, especially in matters of administration and supply, fortification and evacuation; like the S.S. it had become more formidable and more indispensable, with every defeat of German arms. Observers who watched the parallel development of these twin engines of power wondered what would happen when they began to conflict, when Himmler and Bormann, having absorbed or conquered all independent bodies, at last met face to face. In 1943, when Himmler was made Minister of the Interior, that interesting moment had come. Till then the relations between the two men had been excellent; thereafter strong conflicts broke out. The slightest attempts by Himmler to exercise authority outside the S.S. were openly resented by Bormann. In the Provinces several Higher S.S. and Police Leaders thought they could presume on Himmler's new authority and trespass on the preserves of the Gauleiters; they were quickly undeceived. 'Bormann quickly reported such cases to Hitler, and exploited them to fortify his own position. To our surprise (it is Speer who is speaking) it did not take him long to stalemate Himmler as Minister of the Interior.' Such are the advantages of a central position.

H. R. Trevor-Roper, *The Last Days of Hitler* (London: Macmillan, 1965), pp. 41f.

Extract 14

Gladstone's public character up to 1859 was still simple. He was the *vir pietate gravis* of the Oxford High and Broad Churchmen, and the budgetary virtuoso of the politically skilled and earnest section of the aristocracy. Hard reasoning, scholarly aristocrats like Argyll, Carlisle, and Granville, were the people who most fully appreciated the merits of Gladstone's finance: for his successes, useful to them politically, were successes for the qualities they most valued in themselves. He was appalled by frivolity and frivolity was appalled by him. A great Whig lady compared him with Peel for parvenuism:

'. . . something in the tone of his voice and his way of coming into the room that is not aristocratic. In short, he is not frivolous enough for me; if he were soaked in boiling water I do not suppose a single drop of fun would ooze out,

And easy-going men like Clarendon would poke fun at 'our Jesuit' and his 'benevolent nocturnal rambles'. Thus, before 1859, Gladstone was cut off from wide popularity among the Parliamentary class by stiffness and political isolation, and his only source of support was the approbation of an exclusive few, and the votes of the resident electors of the University. Owing to ancient and strict tradition that a University candidate must maintain silence in word and in print during election campaigns, Gladstone was not even able to issue an election address in the years 1847-65. It was an apparently incurable case of political introversion.

Five years later Gladstone wrote, 'I am become for the first time a popular character. As far as I feel justified in appropriating and enjoying any of this popularity, it is on account of what I did, or prevented from being done, in 1859-61 . . .' That is, Gladstone first became popular with the industrialists and with the provincial press, and through the excitement of his contacts with them on what were basically pocket questions, he moved on to the wider popularity of a Dissenting and a working-class hero.

When Gladstone visited Manchester Exchange, he was received with 'loud and repeated cheering'. His popularity in Middlesborough, the Potteries, and the West Riding was equally founded on the hearty good will of the employers. As the member for Bradford said on behalf of his constituents, Bradford was in a more flourishing state than ever previously, and the French treaty caused a great part of that prosperity. Similarly, a Bradford ironmaster wrote, after hearing the Budget of 1860: 'Gladstone was grand last night . . .' Gladstone was not asked but pestered, to stand for industrial constituencies: South Lancashire wanted him in 1861 and subsequently, Leeds asked for him in 1864.

Gladstone was good for trade, but he was good for the provincial press in a quite special degree. For that press, closely tied to radicalism, owed, not a little more or less of trade, but its very existence to Gladstone's paper duties. When Gladstone visited Newcastle in 1862, the arrangements were formally in the hands of the old Liberal oligarchy, but the excitement was stirred up by the Radical party under Cowen, the owner of the penny daily, the *Newcastle Chronicle*, and by Holyoake, who wrote a series of eulogies of Gladstone in that paper. 'The word passed from the newspapers to the workmen,' Holyoake said later, 'and they came out to greet the only English minister who ever gave the people right because it was just they should have it . . . Without him a Free Press in England was impossible . . . If not the first Chancellor of the Exchequer with a conscience, he was the first who was known to have one, and when he went down the Tyne, all the country heard how 20 miles of banks were lined with people who came to greet him.'

> J. Vincent, *The Formation of the Liberal Party, 1857-1868* (London: Constable, 1966), pp. 228-30.

Question on extracts 13 and 14

Many of the characteristics, noted in the previous extracts, are present in these two examples suggesting that there is more in common about the style of leading historians than is sometimes thought. What are these characteristics?

Although the extracts given in the preceding pages are relatively brief they yield a generous amount of information about the qualities of the writer, and this is significant for the student. If his own writing is to be comparably effective it ought to be possible to isolate paragraphs at random from his essays, and to find that the content and expression of each paragraph maintain a consistently high standard. An essay is like a sprint, a book like a marathon, and the shorter form needs a more concentrated intensity of effort. If the student has any notion left that style in essays consists of stretches of narrative lightened at intervals by purple passages then he needs to think again.

In conclusion, it may be encouraging for the student to turn briefly from studying the work of the experts to see the way in which younger historians tackle questions set in Sixth Form work. Two hypothetical examples are given. The first one illustrates the kind of mistakes familiar in schoolboy historical essays. In its negative way this can be very instructive. The second example (extract 16) shows the more sophisticated approach of an able pupil. Both essays are answers to the same question 'Discuss the consequences of the invasion of Silesia by Frederick II.'

Extract 15

'There stands one who will avenge me,' said Frederick William I, the Sergeant-King, ruler of Prussia, in the last moments before his death. The one he was speaking of was his son Frederick, later known to history as Frederick the Great, and although the father had hated and ill-treated his son he still seemed to have some awareness of the ruthless determination, 'the iron hand in the velvet glove' to be found in his son, this verse-maker, flute-player, this admirer of the 'soft' civilisation of the French, this ill-used prince who in spite of all his weaknesses might still be man enough to gain revenge on the Austrians for the wily diplomacy which had robbed Prussia of the lands of Julich Berg promised to Frederick William I in exchange for his approval of the Pragmatic Sanction. If Frederick William could have seen the consequences of the invasion of Silesia which soon followed as Frederick II sought revenge for his father would Frederick William have been so keen on revenge? I doubt it.

When Frederick became the ruler of Prussia in 1740 a war in Europe was very likely because Austria had been weakened by wars in the 1730s, and she owned a large Empire which in the same year fell into the hands of Maria Theresa upon the death of her father Charles VI. Charles VI had secured written promises from most of the European powers that, upon his death, they would not dispute the succession of Maria Theresa but Austria owned too many useful bits of territory for it to be likely that the greedy European powers would keep their word. France was an old rival of Austria and wanted to take advantage of Austrian weakness to extend her influence in Central Europe. In Bavaria the ruling dynasty, the Wittelsbachs, had claims to the title of Holy Roman Emperor themselves, while other German states resented the influence of the Habsburgs over their affairs. An onslaught on Austrian territory seemed certain, whatever had been written on paper, and Frederick II decided to be the first.

The invasion of Silesia went well at first and Glogau and Breslau were quickly captured. Then Frederick wrote letters to Cardinal Fleury, the chief minister of France, and to George II of England to try to win their friendship and to keep them neutral but in fact this was impossible and England went to the aid of Austria since George II decided to keep his word over the Pragmatic Sanction, and France, the sworn enemy of England and her rival in North America and India, joined in the war of the Austrian Succession on Frederick's side, after the latter's somewhat lucky victory over the Austrians at Mollwitz in 1741. Frederick made a secret treaty with the French in which he agreed to support Charles Albert of Bavaria as the new holder of the Imperial crown and to renounce Prussian claims to Julich Berg in return for the French allowing him to retain Lower Silesia. A few months later Frederick made an agreement with the Austrians behind the backs of the French. This was the treaty of Klein-Schnellendorf by which it was agreed that the Austrians after sham operations would withdraw from Lower Silesia and Prussia would abandon the war. A new combined attack by the French, Bavarians, and Saxons led to the capture of Prague, and Frederick, seeing that the Austrians were in great difficulties, broke the Klein-Schnellendorf treaty and attacked Austria again. After winning the battle of Chotusitz Frederick concluded this first Silesian war by making peace with the Austrians and by the terms of the Treaty of Berlin 1742 he received all Silesia except a fringe on the south west.

Austria would never rest so long as Silesia was in Prussian hands and in 1744 her diplomatic activity secured her alliances with England, Sardinia, and Saxony, with the result that Frederick became alarmed and renewed the war. Military operations went quite well but the Prussians lost many men through disease and desertion and were happy to make peace in 1745 by the Treaty of Dresden in which Maria Theresa reluctantly accepted the loss of Silesia for the time being, as she had been obliged to do in the Treaty of Berlin. These treaties mainly concerned Austria and Prussia and it was necessary to have a general peace settlement also involving the other main powers involved. This happened in 1748 and was called the Treaty of Aix-la-Chapelle. As far as Silesia was concerned the other powers agreed to accept the terms of the Treaty of Dresden so Silesia remained Prussia after all. Later there was a further war, the Seven Years War, at the end of which after heavy fighting the Prussians again kept Silesia. Silesia was very useful economically to Prussia, which was a poor country lacking fertility and resources. Apart from this gain Frederick had shown great military skill and strength of character. Inspired by their leader the Prussians had fought well and had Frederick's father lived to see the development of his son's character he would have been very proud, and very well satisfied with the revenge which Frederick took for the slights and snubs which the Sergeant-King had once received at the hands of Austria.

This answer shows much of the characteristic weaknesses of the work of mediocre candidates. It is not hopelessly bad. The writer has a good fund of detailed knowledge. He has a dull style though there are occasional flashes in phrasing and vocabulary which suggest that he is not totally indifferent to the way in which he expresses himself. The major interest, however, is to discover what it is exactly which makes this answer a poor one.

Questions

Paragraph 1
1. The purpose of an introduction is to establish the central theme of the essay clearly and attractively. Does this one do so?
2. Find detailed examples of word wasting and of clichés.
3. Comment on the punctuation.
4. Comment on the phrase 'I doubt it.'

Paragraph 2
1. Is this paragraph relevant?
2. Apart from the question of relevance other features in this paragraph deserve attention. How, for instance, could the first sentence be improved? Comment on the phrase 'useful bits', and on the wording of the last sentence.

Paragraph 3
1. Is this paragraph relevant?
2. 'And' is frequently a weakening word. Show how the writing of this paragraph could be improved by the removal of 'ands', or by substitution for them.

Paragraph 4
1. Comment on 'quite well', and on 'happy' in the second sentence.
2. Comment on the juxtaposition of 'involving' and 'involved' in the third sentence.
3. Improve the fourth sentence.
4. Comment on 'As far as Silesia was concerned' and on 'after all' in the fifth sentence.
5. In the last few sentences the writer attempts to sum up the consequences of the Silesian invasion. How successfully does he do so within the limits of the consequences he has selected?

General question
Apart from faulty expression of ideas what are the major weaknesses of this essay?

Extract 16

The consequence of the Silesian invasion which appealed most strongly to Frederick's hopes was that this single act would establish Prussia as a front-rank European power. 'To make oneself feared and respected by one's neighbours is the acme of high politics' wrote Frederick in his Political Testament. He anticipated too that the campaign would make his own military efficiency apparent to the rest of Europe; the desire for personal achievement, understandable after the humiliations of his childhood, was as strongly marked as his political ambitions for Prussia. Yet the Silesian invasion which seems superficially to be an act of cold-blooded calculation was in reality an act of reckless impulsiveness of dubious value, in spite of the fact that Silesia was seized and successfully held; the consequences which flowed from the invasion, some of them so detrimental to Prussia, had an influence upon European and world history far beyond the narrow vision of Frederick II.

By 1763, with Silesia confirmed as a Prussian possession, and with Austria as war-weary as Prussia herself, Frederick could feel satisfied in some respects with the fruits of aggression. The raw materials and manufacturing wealth of Silesia had fallen into Prussian hands. This new province, the largest and richest Prussian possession, had a prosperous linen industry, undeveloped iron ores, and fertile agricultural lands, a welcome contrast with the impoverished sandy soil of Prussia. Politically, the risk of Silesia falling into Saxon hands, and so linking up Saxony and Poland under joint rule, had been removed; had this come about it might have been Saxony rather than Prussia which would have become the dominant state in north Germany.

Nor does the acquisition of Silesia mark the limit of Frederick's gains. As a military commander he matured remarkably. At Mollwitz in 1741 he had fled the field when the Prussian cavalry was routed, leaving the Prussian infantry under Schwerin to gain the victory. Yet Frederick's victories at Chotusitz and Hohenfriedberg during the War of the Austrian Succession gave early evidence of his latent military skill. The intense military pressure to which Prussia was subjected during the Seven Years War hardened this early talent into genius. His opponents made mistakes, and their attacks were often ill coordinated; nevertheless they had formidable advantages in numbers and in the power to launch attacks upon Prussia from almost every point of the compass. The victories won by Frederick at Rossbach against the French, at Leuthen against the Austrians, and at Liegnitz against a combined Austro-Russian force, were all the more remarkable in view of the odds against him. Even the occasional defeats, as at Kunersdorf, merely showed the toughness and resilience of the Prussian soldiers and their relentless leader. One of the permanent consequences of the long years of war which followed the Silesian invasion was the respect thus earned for the fighting qualities of the Prussian nation, and for the administrative efficiency which enabled the Prussians to make the best use of their resources. The exploits of the Prussian army during these years gave Prussia a military tradition which, though rudely shaken by Napoleon at Jena, survived and gained increasing strength under Bismarck, Kaiser Wilhelm II and Hitler.

It could reasonably be argued that Prussian gains resulting from the Silesian invasion were outweighed by the losses. The acquisition of Silesia had cost Prussia, by Frederick's own estimate, half a million inhabitants. Years of fighting had devastated Silesia itself and the eastern provinces of Prussia. 'The nobility and peasantry' said Frederick 'had been pillaged, ransomed, foraged by so many different armies that only life and miserable rags to cover their nakedness remained to them.' Berlin itself had twice been occupied by enemy troops and in the widespread areas where fighting had taken place the normal processes of administration had broken down exposing the inhabitants to anarchy, famine, disease, and death. Moreover, the cynicism of Frederick's invasion of Silesia had left him without a friend in Europe. Genuine reconciliation with Austria was impossible in Frederick's lifetime. France, Frederick's ally in the War of the Austrian Succession, had been alienated by his tactlessness and duplicity in that war, and fought against him in the Seven Years War. Russia consistently opposed him until Catherine II came to the throne, and though a Russo-Prussian alliance was formed in 1764 the link was tenuous lasting only until 1780. Britain had supported Prussia during the Seven Years War as a matter of expediency but quickly jettisoned the alliance once her aims had been achieved. The German states shared in the universal distrust for Frederick and were jealous of his gains. Frederick had found one way, not necessarily the best one, to establish Prussia as a great power but the cost was prohibitively high.

The consequences of the Silesian invasion had wide implications for European and world history. The heavy involvement of France in the fighting in Europe made easier Britain's task of winning supremacy in the colonial fighting against the French in Canada and India. 'The evils produced by his wickedness,' wrote Macaulay, 'were felt in lands where the name of Prussia was unknown; and, in order that he might rob a neighbour whom he had promised to defend, black men fought on the coast of Coromandel, and red men scalped each other by the Great Lakes of North America.' It might have appealed to Frederick's sardonic sense of humour to know that he thus has some claims to be regarded, unwittingly, as the founder of the British Empire. In Europe one of the most significant consequences of the Silesian attack was that the wars which followed exhausted Prussia, Austria, and France leaving the way wide open for unchallenged Russian domination of eastern Europe; the consequences of this state of affairs reach down into modern times. Once Prussian troops entered Silesia all hope of Austro-Prussian cooperation, which would have given central Europe the stability she has so rarely experienced since, was at an end, until

Bismarck more than a century later was able to patch up their differences. The history of Prussia since 1740 shows with sharp clarity the painful consequences of the Silesian invasion. It was worse than a crime; it was a blunder.

Question

Explain in detail why this answer is superior to the first one.

SUGGESTED ANSWERS

Extract 1

1. A few of the words used are virtually archaic now. 'We should rather be surprised that it had *subsisted* so long.' 'The Byzantine court *beheld* with indifference the disgrace of Rome.' With occasional exceptions, however, the vocabulary used by Gibbon does not differ very much from that employed by modern historians, though he does make greater use of Latinisms. It is in phrases such as 'The rise of a city may deserve as a singular prodigy the reflection of a philosophic mind', or 'Prosperity ripened the principle of decay', or 'The victorious legions violated the majesty of the purple', or 'the salutary event approved in some measure the judgement of Constantine', that a philosophical pose is struck which would be out of place in modern works.

2. The first paragraph consists almost entirely of generalizations, though this is acceptable in the context since Gibbon is here summing up details which he gives elsewhere. What is less justifiable is the philosophic generalization to be found in the second paragraph 'Extreme distress, which unites the virtue of a free people, embitters the factions of a declining monarchy ...' Fortunately the habit of creating phrases of the kind one associates with tear-off calendars is no longer fashionable among historians. Philosophical generalizations have so little validity historically that the tendency nowadays is to avoid them altogether. They are unsound because exceptions are so easy to find. The extreme distress which supposedly 'unites the virtue of a free people' can unite the virtue of an unfree people too, as Gibbon himself might have realized if he had merely cast his mind back to the way in which the Prussian people supported

Frederick in the Seven Years War, in spite of the fact that for much of the war his monarchy could be described as a 'declining' one. Extreme distress can also disunite people as Irish and Scottish history shows. Then too what does Gibbon mean by a 'free people'? Does he mean that they have certain civic privileges, or economic and social freedom? Gibbon's statement is so weakened by imperfect definition and factual inaccuracy that it does not deserve further attention, except as a warning against facile generalization

3. Gibbon's reputation as a stylist is deserved, as this passage shows. Subtle use of the colon and semi-colon, flexibility of vocabulary, and the balanced phrasing and compact expression so strongly marked in the second paragraph, are the major components of his technique as a writer.

4. Gibbon's historical soundness may be vulnerable at times, but there is no doubt of the power and originality of much of his thought. He has the gift, in common with other outstanding historians, of asking new questions about the past and of seeing fresh significance in the course of events. In this passage this approach is evident at two points in particular: first, in his reference to the need to change the emphasis from study of the causes of the fall of the Roman Empire to study of the reasons why it lasted so long as it did; secondly, in his emphasis on the idea that the foundation of Constantinople has little bearing on the decline of Rome.

Extract 2

1. Macaulay's balanced style is strongly in evidence in this extract. The brisk sentences of the second paragraph are completely effective in summing up compactly the early military operations of the war. In the next paragraph the sentences lengthen out as Macaulay marshals his arguments in condemnation of Frederick's actions. A series of short sentences ending in 'The whole world sprang to arms' rounds off this phase of the writing, and leads into the well-known climax where the world-wide effects of Frederick's action are graphically expressed.

2. Phrases such as 'we are compelled to pronounce a condemnation

still more severe', 'to carry the fresh stain of a great crime before the tribunal of his God', 'On the head of Frederick is all the blood which was shed ...' 'The evils produced by his wickedness were felt in lands where the name of Prussia was unknown', all illustrate the way in which Macaulay is apt to use a historical event as a kind of parable on moral behaviour. This approach is identical with the earlier one of Bolingbroke that 'History is philosophy teaching by examples'. The danger with this approach, as later historians have realized, is that it is likely to lead to judgements in which the historian's own feelings play too strong a part. Evidence is more important than opinions, and prejudices, whether national or personal, narrow historical judgement. There is undoubtedly a case for criticizing Frederick's actions; there is also a case for defending them in the context of his times and situation, but no one would imagine this from reading Macaulay's account. Modern historians, more conscious than Macaulay of the scarcity and partiality of historical evidence, and of the limitations of historians themselves, are much more cautious than he was in passing historical judgements.

Extract 3

1. The best which can be said about the metaphors here is that they are ingenious. The obvious weakness is that this passage is overloaded with metaphors. Used so lavishly they lose their effectiveness. Moreover, the metaphors used here are so elaborate that the artificiality of the passage robs the writing of its force.

Extract 4

1. One of the reasons for the greater effectiveness of this second extract from Motley is its much more compact style. Metaphors and similes gain by a certain briskness which adds to the impression that they are arising spontaneously. Brief phrases such as 'Jealousy stuck to him like his shadow' and, to a lesser extent, 'rolling up with strenuous and sometimes despairing arms a dead mountain weight, ever ready to fall back upon and crush him ...' strengthen Motley's writings far more than the long-winded, elaborate metaphors of the first extract.

2. The older generation of historians seldom found it easy to resist moral generalizations. In this extract Motley toys with the generalization that envy is 'more incident to the republican form of government than to other political systems', and the final paragraph is the kind of diatribe which one would be unlikely to find in the work of a modern historian. Both these moral generalizations would be difficult to substantiate; neither lends itself to verification by evidence, and the absolute condemnation of envy in the last paragraph could be applied with equal validity to any of the less creditable human emotions.

3. The strong feature of the writing here is the way in which arguments are advanced in quick succession, with few digressions until the final climax is reached. The use of short sentences and economy of expression are strongly marked in the first half of the extract particularly. In essay writing the short space available makes the capacity to develop an argument swiftly of pre-eminent importance, and though the young historian will not want to imitate the rather dated language of Motley the simple yet varied sentence structure used here is a useful model of style.

Extract 5

1. Overstatements easily arise when, as has happened here, the writer abandons any attempt at objectivity. Phrases such as 'They had no earthly object emphatically none', 'In tough contact with reality (they) had learnt better than the great and the uneducated the difference between truth and lies', 'spiritual rulers over them alike powerful and imbecile', 'a little band of enthusiasts, armed only with truth and fearlessness', are so sweeping, whether in praise or condemnation, that they undermine confidence in Froude's judgement.

2. The danger is making a contrast, in this instance between the enthusiasts and the conservatives, is that the unsound or inexperienced historian is apt to exaggerate the difference between the two sides, partly because sharp contrast can add to the effectiveness of literary expression, and partly because he may genuinely, and generally wrongly, see contending sides in history as wholly good or wholly evil.

3. Froude's sympathy for the London Protestants is blatantly obvious, to an extent which makes his description unacceptable as sound historical writing. His own strong sympathy for the simplification of religious forms is very marked in the last part of the extract. The weakness in this style of writing lies in the attempt to appeal to emotions, rather than to allow verified facts to speak for themselves.

4. In a literary sense the contrast between the London Protestants and the forces of conservatism opposed to them is effectively made. Phrases are neatly balanced against each other, often by the use of semi-colons. The long quotation blends opportunely with his argument and the final sentence works up to an effective climax.

Extract 6

1. Mannered writing of this kind does not automatically show a deficiency in the writer's historical skill, but it carries with it dangers of exaggeration, and its artificiality can be irritating. The phrasing is frequently pretentious, 'like a great wind blowing off an unknown shore' (a simile which fits in none too happily with the concept involved in the writer's reference to 'the full prose life of men'), 'by a secret ordering of the mysteries of birth he had been created with more in him of the divine than any training can give', 'his mind was like a vast sea-cave, filled with the murmur of dark waters at flow and the stirring of nature's forces, lit here and there by streaks of glorious sunshine bursting in through crevices hewn at random in its rugged sides'. Pursuit of literary effect leads to sweeping generalizations, too, such as 'The man who loved Italy as even she has seldom been loved', 'He had all the distinctive qualities of the hero, in their highest possible degree, and in their very simplest form'. 'Courage and endurance without limit . . .'

2. Within the limits previously indicated there is no doubt that Trevelyan was an outstanding literary technician. His use of long sentences builds up an impressive momentum, and the flow of his thought is skilfully maintained by the balanced phrasing so evident in the second half of the extract, by the use of semi-colons, and,

occasionally, by repetition ('so ignorant of despair and doubt, so potent to overawe his enemies').

3. Historical comparisons are twice used. First, in the reference to Cromwell and secondly in the reference to Moltke. Both comparisons arise naturally in their contexts. Comparisons of this kind give some indication of the historian's ability to integrate his knowledge, and are useful in enlarging the approach of writer and reader to the past.

4. This is a good instance of the greater virtues of style which can be achieved by use of the concrete instead of the abstract phrase.

5. Trevelyan refers to Garibaldi's 'child-like simplicity that often degenerated into folly' and to the fact that Garibaldi was 'but dimly enlightened'. Yet even these weaknesses are made to appear as if they were virtues, and the tone of the passage otherwise is one of uncritical admiration for Garibaldi. It bears more resemblance to hero-worship than history.

Extract 7

1. Examples of balanced phrasing can be found throughout the whole extract but an early example occurs in the use of repetition 'so powerful and so severe a mind, so stern in his individual life, a monk of the monks, a dogmatist of the dogmatists ...'. Balance is also secured by contrast. 'Austerity was part of the ordinary religious type of the time ...' writes Church; then after some exemplification he continues 'But Anselm's almost light-hearted cheerfulness ... formed a combination with personal austerity with which his age was not familiar.' Church makes frequent use of contrast between the general trends of thought of the time and Anselm's individualistic contribution. The massing of phrases is an object lesson in the swift delineation of character; the sentence referring to Anselm's 'light-hearted cheerfulness, his winning and informal nature ...' is a good instance. The words and phrases used are frequently striking in themselves, 'a dogmatist of dogmatists' 'his temper of moderation and good sense' 'the vein of quaint and unceremonious amusement'. As one would expect in well-constructed

writing of this type semi-colons are frequently used. The sentence 'The days of the great preachers were at hand; but they had not yet come.' illustrates the point well.

2. Neat scholarly allusion is a feature of Church's writing and shows how depth of knowledge can be deftly used. Phrases such as 'the great Conqueror was austere ...', 'a talent for simple and natural explanation which reminds the reader sometimes of Luther or Latimer—more truly perhaps of St. François de Sales and of the vein of quaint and unceremonious amusement running through some of the later Italian works of devotion', show this aspect of the historian's mind at work.

3. It may seem that Church has fallen into the familiar trap of accepting the better qualities of his central character too uncritically. On the other hand the references to documentary evidence are reasonably specific. Church mentions the homilies found among Anselm's works and the last reference from Eadmer is sufficiently full to show that there is sound evidence for the remarks Church makes about Anselm's special gifts as a religious leader.

Extract 8

1. Overcoming the disadvantage of hindsight is an essential part of historical training. One aspect of this training is to recognize that characters need to be judged by the standards of their contemporaries and not by those of the historian. This is very ably argued in the extract. The convincing nature of the argument comes mainly from the abundantly sound sense shown, but the range of ideas and their controlled expression firmly buttress the arguments.

2. The difference between 'He believed war to be right' and 'he believed in his own cause' is slight, possibly non-existent, but otherwise this last sentence perfectly caps the argument, and the terse 'he accomplished it' is a good example of a strong finish.

Extract 9

1. Even this brief extract shows something of Maitland's excep-

tional gifts as a historian. There is, in the first place, a readiness to scrutinize a 'label' term—the feudal system—and to question whether the assumptions made about it, which gain in strength by repetition, have any substance in fact. In attacking conventional notions about the feudal system his reliance upon primary sources is strongly in evidence throughout; moreover his knowledge of the authorities is more than a matter of a fleeting reference. 'In all his (Coke's) books, unless I am mistaken, there is no word about the feudal system'. 'For "a feudal system" we must turn to a contemporary of his, that learned and laborious antiquary, Sir Henry Spelman.' 'The new learning was propagated among English lawyers by Sir Martin Wright'. What is impressive and revealing in phrases of this kind is the manner in which, without a false note, they indicate a familiarity with sources which it would be difficult to match. It lends some support to the theory that the capacity of a historian is as apparent in his asides as in his main theme. Maitland's presentation of his argument about the feudal system is almost as striking as the argument itself. If the hypothetical examiner whom Maitland mentions had been confronted in practice with the brilliant and well-substantiated reasoning to be found in this extract it would have been one of those occasions when it is the examinee who enlarges the understanding of the examiner. The historical width and paradoxical insight of the last few sentences round off a remarkably able piece of historical writing, original in concept, persuasive in argument, and perfectly balanced and controlled in a literary sense.

2. There is little to criticize as the previous comments suggest. The only weaknesses are that the writing verges towards a conversational style at times, and could occasionally be sharpened by word removal. The opening sentence is one of the few instances where Maitland is too wordy. It could be revised to read 'In this country any talk of a feudal system is a comparatively new thing; we do not hear of a feudal system until long after feudalism had ceased to exist.' His method of presenting the argument necessarily involves frequent use of personal pronouns but, at the risk of being hypercritical, the writing might gain in sharpness if these pronouns were less frequently used, particularly in the first half where they do not always add to the effectiveness of the ideas being conveyed.

Extract 10

1. To be effective quotations need to be apposite, interesting, and from a reliable source; they also need to be fitted smoothly into their context in a literary sense. All these conditions are abundantly fulfilled in this extract. The quotations arise so naturally in their context that the reader is hardly aware of the skill with which they are being used, perhaps the best tribute of all to a writer.

2. The outstanding feature of this extract, as descriptive writing, is the formidable array of specific knowledge which the writer brings to bear upon her theme. It is temptingly easy in descriptive passages to rely on undisciplined imagination and vague surmises. By contrast this extract shows the power of factual certainty. Every comment made is justified by abundant historical evidence. Most questions set for students in schools and universities test the analytical rather than the descriptive powers of the writer, but occasionally there are questions on social life which lend themselves to the type of writing illustrated in the extract; a flair for soundly based descriptive writing deserves consideration as one of the essential skills of historical writing.

Extract 11

1. This introduction to the reign of George I is instructive in two respects. It demonstrates how deftly a complex period of history can be summarized by an accomplished historian; the long but controlled sentences here serve the writer's purpose admirably. Secondly, the writer has made a shrewd selection of the events from the seventeenth century most likely to have been influential on men's minds in 1714. So often the 'historical background' introduction is mechanically used, and its relevance to the events which follow is not made plain; this extract shows the virtues of significant selection of facts.

Extract 12

1. The dualism of Peel's character particularly invites the setting of

point against point, but the historian often finds himself confronted by the need for a 'judicial' summing-up of arguments he has advanced and this extract provides a good model for him. The most marked feature of style is the way in which semi-colons are so freely and effectively used as the writer skilfully builds up the contrasting sides of Peel's character. Occasional repetition of words 'Ingrowing virtues have a trick of developing ingrowing vices', 'the world needed ... fewer ordinary politicians. But politics ... is made up of ordinary men.', adds force to this kind of writing, though it is a device to be used sparingly, otherwise the style becomes theatrical. The balancing of phrase against phrase is conspicuously present throughout. The last phrase, 'he commanded their respect but rarely devotion', illustrates it perfectly.

2. In general a semi-colon is a substitute for 'and'; if both are present one is presumably superfluous. There are sentences in this extract where the omission of the 'and' after a semi-colon would sharpen the impact of the writing. 'The need for self-protection easily enlists less amiable qualities on its side; *and* of these Peel had his full share.' On the other hand in the sentence 'Only a person of great humility could have held Peel's standards and retained complete humanity; and Peel was not humble' the presence of the 'and' avoids the jerkiness of style which is apt to arise when semi-colons are too lavishly used.

Extract 13

The characteristic features are:

1. The reliance on primary sources for evidence.

2. The skilful blending of quotations and text.

3. The use of semi-colons to achieve a forceful style.

4. Economy of phrase, 'indispensable, indefatigable, and ubiquitous'.

5. The gift, springing from a wide vocabulary and literary skill, for unexpected words and phrasing, 'to attain to any singularity of

position in his counsels' 'having thumped their tubs and blown their trumpets obstreperously'.

6. Repetition, 'the sole custodian of Hitler's secrets, the sole channel for his orders, the sole method of approach ...'

7. The strong concluding sentence.

Extract 14

Although there are naturally individual differences the resemblances in style between Extract 13 and Extract 14 are numerous; comparisons between these two extracts and those given from other historians would also show considerable overlap in stylistic features. In this extract the characteristics are:

1. The reliance on primary sources for evidence.

2. The skilful blending of quotations and text.

3. The use of short sentences rather than semi-colons to give sharpness to the style, though colons are sometimes used.

4. The gift for striking words and phrasing 'the *vir pietate gravis* of the Oxford High', 'the budgetary virtuoso', 'an apparently incurable case of political introversion'.

5. Repetition, 'He was appalled by frivolity and frivolity was appalled by him'. 'Gladstone was good for trade, but he was good for the provincial press in a quite special degree'.

6. A strong conclusion achieved here by use of a quotation.

Extract 15

Paragraph 1

1. This introduction fails in its purpose. The central theme of the essay is the consequences of the Silesian invasion. The writer's

judgement on this issue should be established as quickly as possible. Except for the vague implication at the end of the paragraph that the Silesian invasion had some harmful effects for Prussia, the writer of this essay has ignored the main issue. The death-bed scene and the description of Frederick's characteristics before he became King are irrelevant.

2. The writer has not only undermined his essay by irrelevance but also by his partiality for padding. Allusive phrases can be an asset in giving depth to an answer, but they need to be relevant, significant, and brief. The allusions used here have none of these qualities. Examples are the phrases 'later known to history as Frederick the Great', and the long section in parenthesis about Frederick beginning at '. . . ruthless determination' and continuing at least to '. . . ill-used prince'. Clichés occur in 'ruthless determination', 'the iron hand in the velvet glove', 'wily diplomacy', 'might be man enough to gain revenge' and clichés do not become more forgivable by protecting them with inverted commas, as the writer does here with his 'iron hand' reference. Inverted commas thus used merely indicate that the writer is half-aware that he is using a cliché, but that he is too lazy to find an alternative.

3. The second sentence is overburdened with allusions and this has extended its length unnaturally; so too has the accumulation of subordinate clauses. The sentence needs to be sub-divided into manageable units by the use of semi-colons and full-stops.

4. The personal pronoun is generally obtrusive and superfluous in an essay. The writer's doubt could easily be conveyed by recasting the previous sentence 'If Frederick William . . . it is doubtful whether he would have been so keen on revenge.'

Paragraph 2

1. No. The diplomatic situation in 1740 has no relevance to the consequences of the Silesian invasion.

2. The sentence is grammatically correct but clumsily constructed. It could be rephrased thus, 'When Frederick became the ruler of Prussia a war in Europe was very likely. Austria had been weakened by wars in the 1730s; she owned a large Empire which in 1740 fell into the hands of Maria Theresa upon the death of her father Charles VI. 'Useful bits' is the kind of weak phrase apt to appear

in the work of young writers with a limited vocabulary and no sense of style. The last sentence illustrates the same weaknesses; in this instance it has produced a loosely constructed sentence without any merit except the unintentional one that its ambiguity makes it mildly amusing.

Paragraph 3

1. The writer has at last achieved a minor degree of relevance. The military and diplomatic events of 1740-2 were undoubtedly consequences of the Silesian invasion, though not the most important ones. The writer's sense of relevance is of a very limited, literal, and immature kind.

2. Many variants are possible and there is no point in giving one rather than another here. The increased impact gained by reducing weak connecting words to a minimum, generally by substituting full stops or semi-colons, will be self-evident if the reader compares the original with his own version. It is worth noting, in passing, that the removal of 'in fact' in 'but in fact this was impossible', and of 'somewhat' in 'the latter's somewhat lucky victory over the Austrians', would also strengthen the writing.

Paragraph 4

1. 'Quite well' and 'happy' are not flagrant examples of colloquialisms, but they are semi-colloquial, and have a vagueness, naïveté, and a touch of inaccuracy which are more common in the work of weak candidates than outright blunders.

2. Unintentional repetition of words is an ugliness in style. Sometimes it springs from writing at speed; more often it is caused by poverty of vocabulary and carelessness over sentence construction.

3. 'This agreement, the Treaty of Aix-la-Chapelle, was concluded in 1748.'

4. 'As far as Silesia is concerned' is a superfluous phrase. Even if it were not it is an ugly expression, like 'as regards ...', 'regarding ...': they have a strong resemblance to business letter jargon and ought to be avoided. 'After all' in this context is merely padding, and ought to be discarded.

5. The retention of Silesia by Prussia, and its economic value, are

relevant issues; so too is the development of Frederick's character in that his conduct of the war won European respect for Prussian military capacity. On the other hand, the 'revenge' theme of the last sentence is of little, if any, historical significance, and therefore makes a weak end to the essay. The only merit it has is that it refers back to the idea advanced by the writer in his introduction that the Silesian war was undertaken to avenge Prussian diplomatic set-backs at Austrian hands; if this were a correct, relevant, and important issue then a reference back to it in the concluding paragraph would be an asset, but this is not so in this instance.

General Question

The two major weaknesses are irrelevance and narrowness of outlook. It takes the writer two paragraphs to come to the point. When he eventually does so his view of the consequences of the Silesian invasion is virtually limited to a description of the fighting, and of the treaty arrangements by which Prussian possession of Silesia was confirmed. There are vague fleeting references to Silesia's economic value, and to Frederick's military skill, but a comparison with the second essay on the same theme will show the restricted historical ability of the first writer.

Extract 16

The merits of this much stronger answer on the same theme are as follows:

1. The powerful sense of relevance. The first sentence, neatly backed by an apposite quotation from Frederick, goes straight to the point. Throughout the essay clear relevant arguments are sustained. The precise economic and political advantages of the seizure of Silesia, the influence of the wars on Prussian military tradition, on European and world history, are all shown. The writer has a good knowledge of detail but rightly uses it for its proper function in essays of illustrating argument; this avoids the trap into which weaker writers fall of producing a mass of detailed narrative, often of marginal relevance or none.

2. Width of approach. This is evident in the very wide view taken of the consequences of the invasion in terms of Prussian, European, and world history in the eighteenth century. But the writer has not confined himself to the immediate contemporary effects. By neat allusive reference, to the activities of Bismarck and Hitler for instance, he has shown awareness of the fact that the Silesian invasion had consequences reaching down into the twentieth century.

3. Balanced judgement. The writer deals fairly with the conventional judgement that Frederick's action established Prussia as a major European power; at the same time he is not blind to the heavy economic and political cost to Prussia of the Silesian invasion.

4. Sense of style. The sentence structure is well controlled, and it is notable how semi-colons help in this process. A few well-chosen quotations, deftly blended with comment, are given. The writer has a mature vocabulary. He also has at times a flair for creating a striking phrase: the reference to Frederick's unwitting part in founding the British Empire is one instance of this; so too is the final sentence which has the additional merit that it rounds off the essay decisively.